DAVE A. CORNELIUS, DM

JCWALK PUBLISHING

Belonging and Healing

Images inspired and provided by Dave Cornelius, DM

JCWALK Publishing
ISBN: 978-0-9963936-6-9 (eBook); 978-0-9963936-7-6 (Print).
PRINTED IN THE UNITED STATES OF AMERICA

Extend the Story: www.BelongingHealingBook.com

CONTENTS

DEDICATION

The matriarchs in my life were foundational and helped to shape various aspects of my life. I give dedication to my mother, Celie E. Brow; grandmother Verni Anthony; and great-grandmother Louisa George. Each placed a brick in my life that helped me grow as a person. They saw the rough edges in me and began smoothing out those areas to make me better.

My uncle Vere Anthony left his earthly body to live forevermore in the hearts and minds of the people that he touched and made better. I am one of those people, so I am forever grateful for his counsel when I was on my way to my first year in college. I told him that I wanted to focus on music as a major and computer science as a minor, and he said, "Turn the priorities around. I taught you how to play the guitar so you have that natural gift for music, but if you get a skill in computers, which are the future, you will be able to create a positive career and still do music." That advice allowed me to thrive in the technology field and use my musical skills creatively.

Much love to my wife, Carmen; son, Dave; daughter, Devan; and grandson, Aden. Our belonging and healing journey will ensure generational growth in our family.

Special thanks to my sisters Lateefah, Cleo, Debbie, Dessirie, and Terry and my brother, George, for participating in the Zoom family gatherings to increase our sense of belonging and healing during the COVID-19 global pandemic. We have become closer to our mother's hope of being family. To my nieces (Talita, Keetwana, Demyra, Celida, Kayanna, Terrianna, and Jerrise) and nephews (Phanon and Yan) who showed up in the virtual family gathering to support our family becoming closer and connecting generationally. Hail up to my B-in-law Kaunda (Charles) for belonging to our tribe: much respect.

Special shout out and thank you to the men and women serving on the frontlines during the COVID-19 pandemic who supported our communities finding belonging and healing. The COVID-19 pandemic effect has been devastating as an estimated 14.9 million people globally lost their lives, with one million in the United States.

To the healers working to bring belonging and healing in our communities and business organizations so that we are not limited by race, gender, religious affiliation, other life choices, and socio-economic gaps. We are stronger together than being separated by ideology. The healers include professional coaches, psychotherapists, DEI evangelists, and others building a better environment for psychological and physical safety.

Renholdt "Rookie" Jackson, thank you for creating a space for young men and women to grow their creative energies in the Police Athletic League (PAL) program. The space to allow our musical and many other creative energies to thrive lives with me today.

Danny Cornelius, thank you for your guidance as the varsity basketball coach at Central High School on St. Croix USVI. You were a positive influence on many young men who encountered your intensity and good humor. RIP.

Thank you to Theodore Brow Jr., my stepfather, who exposed me as a 12-year-old to entrepreneurship by allowing me to work at the Brow Soda factory in Frederiksted, St. Croix USVI. The experience and knowledge remains with me today.

ACKNOWLEDGEMENTS

A special thank you to Tracy Treacy, founder of D & S Healing Center, for sharing her knowledge in the *KnolShare with Dr. Dave* podcasts on the topics of belonging and healing covered in this book. Tracy is my lifelong sister, friend, and partner in healing. We found a project that we can collaborate on to bring about healing for others.

Gratitude to Nobantu Mpotulo from Ubuntu Coaching in South Africa for sharing her knowledge about the practice of Ubuntu. Nobantu helped me understand the foundational premise that Ubuntu is the way of being, a way of life that takes into consideration the importance of interconnection, the importance of working with others, and the importance of seeing the good in others.

Earl Cobb has been a wonderful connection who brought inspiration to the work that I do for my community. His encouraging words were, "The book should help many deserving people and suitably support your outstanding and heartfelt mission." I am very grateful to be associated with such greatness.

For almost a year during the COVID-19 pandemic, Michael, Jessica, and I collaborated on workforce development innovations for under-estimated communities. Those were welcoming connections during the gray days of being isolated and limited to virtual interactions. It was great connecting in person after the restrictions were lifted.

Cherie Silas and Alex Kudinov of Tandem Coaching Academy, you are wonderful learning facilitators who helped me increase my professional and organizational coaching capabilities.

Alicia McLain, keep rocking the work you are doing in the professional and organizational coaching community. Your voice is essential.

FOREWORDS

Ervin (Earl) Cobb

After retiring from a thirty-five-year corporate career, which I started as a young engineer with Honeywell Information Systems, designing mainframe computers, and ended with me spending the last fifteen years as a technology and management executive with Motorola, Inc. and the Wells Fargo Bank, I began to coach and write about the core fundamentals of organizational leadership. To date, I am proud to share that I have written and published more than ninety books and articles that have reached and contributed to the leadership development of professionals around the globe.

While living in Tucson, Arizona, in 2015-2019, I published two of my bestselling books on leadership development. They both target project management professionals and led me to become a member of the Tucson Chapter of the Project Management Institute. It was during my time in Tucson when I had the opportunity to meet Dr. Dave Cornelius and begin my professional collaboration with him. I also must admit that it was through my collaboration with Dr. Dave that I began to entirely understand the power of *"the sense of belonging."*

During this period, I closely observed the tremendous amount of focus and work that Dave has invested in himself, his clients, and others around him by harnessing and positively utilizing the transformative power of *belonging* within individuals and organizations. I am delighted to see that his years of study, writing, lectures, coaching, and numerous podcast interviews have culminated into the amazingly straightforward and glaringly insightful book you are about to read.

By coupling the sense of *belonging* with a sincere focus on the diverse level of *healing* that may be required to obtain this state of being, Dr. Dave has written a book that not only *informs,* but also has the potential to significantly *improve* the overall performance of individuals and organizations.

Belonging and Healing should be viewed as your opportunity to meet and begin your professional collaboration with Dr. Dave and to begin your journey to not just understanding the power of *the sense of belonging,* but putting it to work to improve yourself and your organization.

I honestly believe that this is a book packed with messages that are ripe for the times.

Today, more than ever, the world needs more extraordinary and awesome people. Through my association with Dr. Dave and the respect I have gained for his wisdom and benevolence, I am convinced that he is the right person to help you create your *awesomeness.*

Ervin (Earl) Cobb is a retired Motorola and Wells Fargo Bank executive. Earl is a distinguished leadership development coach, speaker, and author. He is currently the CEO and managing partner of Richer Life, LLC.

Cherie Silas

As a former executive and International Coaching Federation Master Certified Coach and European Mentoring and Coaching Council Accredited Supervisor and Master Coach who has also been in a bi-racial family since 1989, I have had a firsthand view of the need for belonging and healing happening in the world around me.

I first met Dave as a fellow agilist in the agile community and later had the opportunity to help him develop his competency as a professional coach through my work at the company I founded in 2017, Tandem Coaching Academy. It was at this time that I was introduced to the work that Dave is doing highlighting the need for belonging and healing across racial lines.

The work he has done in this book is a refreshing approach on the important topic of DEI and introduces the fascinating practice of Ubuntu, which is a spiritual healing journey and has great potential to help many people peel off the effects of not belonging in a society where all humans should be honored as they hold a valuable and unique space in the world.

I am thankful to Dave for the work he is doing in this area and believe that you will benefit from the content of this book.

Cherie Silas, MCC, is the founder and managing director of Tandem Coaching Academy.

Alicia McLain

As an African American woman who grew up in Orange County in the '70s when it was considerably less welcoming to black and brown people and had a twenty-five-plus year career in tech and today is a full-time RVer and nomad, for me, belonging has been more than a footnote for my life's story to date.

Over the course of my career, my professional crusade has been in service to belonging, through the work that I've done around Diversity, Equity, and Inclusion. My corporate work leading diversity teams locally and internationally, my work as an individual contributor up through executive positions in tech, and today, my work as an executive leadership coach all come down to belonging and acceptance, and that work starts with self.

As an ICF coach, I work with corporate, community, and civic leaders at all levels from C-suite to individual contributors. My coaching specialty is around positive intelligence and mental fitness, the key that unlocks the patterns of our thinking that separates us from others, triggers us, and sabotages our success. This work is a gift, and it leads people to self-acceptance. Healing can only happen with acceptance. The part the mind plays in belonging and healing is that connection is found in the right hemisphere of the brain. It's only through this mental fitness that we can build the bridges that reach toward our fellow humans, to build those bridges and start the healing.

Dave and I met in the cozy agile community of agile coaches in Southern California. As people of color, he and I gravitated to each other to find a sense of belonging, community, and support. What has always struck me about

Dave is his compassion and commitment to humanizing the work we do. While others are talking about frameworks, he leads with the human side of this work. I'll also say, a bit tongue in cheek, that I've always been amazed at how many more hours he seems to have in his day than the average bear. He's incredibly accomplished in his education with his PhD as well as professionally and personally, and he seems to do it all with great patience and grace.

From my experience with Dave, this work comes as no surprise. Humanity, belonging, and healing are themes, patterns, and what are obvious pillars in his mission. I appreciate the introduction of new ideas, concepts, and theories around Ubuntu that Dave has brought forth in this work.

What gets in the way of belonging is fear. Dave's work serves as a guide to building the awareness of this and moving past it to lean into healing. It takes courage to do this work. This quote resonates for me as I think of Dave's compassionate and human expression in this book. "When I dare to be powerful—to use my strength in the service of my vision, then it becomes less and less important whether I am afraid." - Audre Lorde

Dave's work in this book inspires curiosity, makes connections, and is a step in the direction of building bridges with self, teams, and in organizations. I've had several clips and takeaways that sparked exploration for me, and for that, I'm grateful. This book is absolutely an invitation to explore. You'll appreciate the journey you take from the prompts and introductions in this book.

Alicia R. McLain is the founder and principal executive leadership coach for her company that's home-based in San Diego: Operational Innovations. Alicia is a distinguished leadership development coach, inspirational public keynote speaker, and trainer.

INTRODUCTION

COVID-19 pressed the stop button on our world's activities and made us pause for a moment to take notice of the harm done to each living being on this planet. If there was ever a time to reimagine who we are and how we can make things better, this is that moment. A moment to co-create a vision of belonging and a time to find healing for the trauma experienced throughout our lives. This is a journey that asks for thoughtfulness and experimentation to learn and grow. I want to begin with the destination in mind and go on a journey from the trauma that we experienced to the healing that makes us whole, so that we can find our place of belonging. Belonging is a basic human need. It's an important part of who we are and how we find identity. The language of belonging is a tone of invitation, a voice of acceptance, and the sound of empathy.

In concert, healing is needed to create space for growth and abundance thinking, removing the impediments that distract our focus from the true opportunity of living in the moments of our best self. As you move along the path of healing, there will be generative and limiting healing experiences.

Generative healing will help to produce living options that enable participation in status quo activities and help discover new ways of thriving. Many professional sports athletes experience generative healing after going through a traumatic physical injury and are able to return to the same level of play or better. NBA player Kevin Durant (KD) experienced severe physical trauma to his Achilles tendon and is back contributing to his team after generative healing. Generative healing can be a difficult journey, but the resilience of the mind, body, and spirit amplifies the path to becoming whole.

Limiting healing often reduces the possibility for growth because our gaze is too focused on the trauma. The mind, body, and spirit are clouded with what is not possible. Sometimes the trauma is too great to overcome. We see the struggle in people recovering from substance abuse, fighting the good fight but unable to sustain recovery. There is a mantra in recovery groups of "keep coming back," which creates the sense of belonging and connection.

Belonging and healing is possible in organizations when the organization is viewed through the lens of having human attributes. The human attributes may include a brain, emotions, mobility, intuition, and much more, and they have the intrinsic need to be sustainable and grow. The organization with a brain has the ability to learn and grow over time, which supports the ability to establish a strategy for the belonging experience and apply practices to implement the belonging strategy.

Belonging and healing are prerequisites for diversity, equity, and inclusion (DEI) to be effective. DEI will be more accepted when belonging belongs to everyone and healing can take place in the minds, bodies, and spirit of the organization's people. Belonging and healing existed way before the concept of DEI, as these human needs were not inventions born in corporate America. Global Industry Analysts Inc. (2021) estimated the global DEI market would be US$9.3 billion in the year 2022, and it is projected to reach a revised size of US$15.4 billion by 2026, growing at a CAGR of 12.6% over the analysis period. How much is belonging estimated to grow? Research with financial projections was not available to demonstrate the growth of belonging. Kennedy and Jain-Link (2021) stated, "While a lack of belonging is the challenge, building it is a crucial strategy for healing and for galvanizing support for all DEI work."

If belonging and healing becomes a cornerstone for organizations, then perhaps the 47 million people resigning from their jobs in the United States during the Great Resignation (Parker and Horowitz, 2022) would be less. People may stay longer at their jobs for more than the average of four years in my opinion. Innovation and productivity would be greater, and employees would have a greater share in corporate profits.

The topics shared and discussed in this book serve the individuals and groups working in professional coaching, organizational coaching, and DEI. Other practitioners may apply the concepts and practices to help improve belonging and healing in organizations and communities.

BELONGING AND HEALING - UBUNTU

When you want to go fast, you go alone; when you want to go far, you go together.
– African proverb

Ubuntu is a Xhosa word originating from a South African philosophy that encapsulates aspirations to live life well together. It represents a universal human bond that guides us to believe that I am only because you are. Archbishop Desmond Tutu said, "A person is a person through other persons." The principle enlightens us to see everyone as fully human, connected by humanity, so that we are able to treat others as having immense worth. By embracing the philosophy of Ubuntu and living it out in daily life, it's possible for us to overcome division and be stronger together in a world where wise people build bridges and not walls.

The fundamental meaning of Ubuntu is that things we learn and experience are based on relationships we have with other people. People have meaning because we learn to love others as we love ourselves. Each interaction is a gift and enriches our lives. Ubuntu is an African spiritual healing journey. Ubuntu is about community, integrity, and honesty; it's really the spirit of togetherness.

The late Archbishop Tutu and former South African President Nelson Mandela used the principles of Ubuntu to bring the South African nation together after the inhumane and genocidal practices of apartheid. The Truth and Reconciliation Commission (TRC) of South Africa healed a nation that could easily have been engulfed in revenge and bloodshed for the violence that had been enacted against the original people of South Africa. However, Tutu's vision of using Ubuntu to heal the racial and tribal violence demonstrated how a restorative system, over a retributive form of justice, is possible. If a nation that lived through decades of gross injustice, hatred, and violence can find healing with Ubuntu, then it is possible that belonging and healing can be restored in other communities.

I am moved to believe that Ubuntu was also present in the enslaved African peoples' spirit in the United States after the Emancipation Proclamation. Evans (2022) found former President Abraham Lincoln believed that the former slaves would overrun the country with violence, and he said, "Your race suffer from living among us, while ours suffer from your presence ... It is better for us both, therefore, to be separated." It is plausible that the spirit of Ubuntu allowed the enslaved African people to see their former captors through their own humanity and not retaliate with violence.

How can these concepts create a community of belonging and healing? Start with empathy. Empathy is the ability to visualize another person's journey and perceive that you can walk in their shoes and footsteps. Empathy is not a natural state of mind, and it requires mindfulness to have a stance of identifying with other people's experiences and the world that we inhabit. The reality is that you may not be able to visualize another person's journey or walk in their shoes because you cannot relate to their context.

If you have never experienced poverty, it is difficult to understand the meaning of going to bed hungry for one week. If you have never experienced sexual objectification as many women have, it is difficult to walk in her shoes. Even if we are unable to see what it is like to walk in the footsteps of another human being, the effort of going through the experience of showing empathy is what matters most.

Ubuntu Over Narcissism

Ubuntu trumps narcissism. Ubuntu by design is about equality between each person and not one person being superior to the other. Archbishop Tutu said Ubuntu "is about the essence of being human; my humanity is caught up, bound up, inextricably, with yours. When I dehumanize you, I inexorably dehumanize myself." Nadra Nittle (2021) found that narcissism is a psychiatric disorder characterized by a lack of empathy, superficial charm, pathological lying, a grandiose sense of self-worth, manipulation, and other traits. Narcissism contradicts the goals of Ubuntu, which is about oneness between people and not for the edification of the individual. The narcissistic character is embraced and celebrated as a hero in most organizations. The streaming series *Super Pumped* and *WeCrashed* about the leaders of Uber and WeWork, respectively, are an example of narcissistic leaders putting themselves over the people during the startup periods in those companies. Women and other marginalized groups of people were severely treated as less than equals in the stories told about the leaders of Uber and WeWork.

Ubuntu may not be enough to neutralize the narcissistic behaviors affecting members of an organization. If narcissism is treated as a psychiatric disorder, then those individuals afflicted with the disorder may need individual counseling and to potentially even be removed temporarily to allow the organization to pursue belonging and healing in the group. Ubuntu can be the practice to create oneness to remedy the harm done to members of the organization.

Ubuntu Over Microaggression

Microaggressions are subtle statements and actions that imply a bias against a person based on gender, race, religion, or sexual orientation. The microaggression behavior can be intentional or unintentional, both creating harm to the targeted individuals or groups. The message signals that the target is a lesser human being and invalidates the relevance of lived experiences. Verbal and nonverbal microaggressions are equally harmful. Racial microaggression examples include statements like:

- "When I look at you, I don't see color."
- "There is only one race, which is the human race."
- "You speak such good English."

Gender microaggression examples include:

- Women walking down the street receiving catcalls from men.
- Comments targeted at women that state, "You are so emotional" or "She is so aggressive."

Microaggressions are not always loud and in your face and can be subtle in the form of nonverbal communications that include lack of eye contact and ignoring the existence of a marginalized group of people. Microaggressions can have devastating economic impacts and are manifested when a person is denied a job or promotion because of gender, race, religion, or sexual orientation.

If we were able to see each other through the lens of Ubuntu, there would be more equality and diversity in top leadership roles. White men make up 30% of the United States population but hold the majority of key positions, including the following (Srikanth, 2021):

- 40% of tenured positions in higher education.
- 62% of the House of Representatives.

- 62% of the U.S. Senate.
- 90% of Forbes 500 executive CEO-level positions.
- 67% of public school superintendents.
- 99% of athletic team owners.
- 99% of U.S. presidents.

With such a disparity of white men holding key roles in the most important institutions in our society, the reality is there is a limited point of view to see non-white men and women as equals. The practice of Ubuntu is a remedy to this disparity to encourage us to go far together and remove the microaggressions that ultimately limit progress of non-white people.

Ubuntu Brings Gratitude

Practicing the habit of equality with people in your family, community, and organization will lead to gratitude that relieves the stresses of being overwhelmed by narcissism, microaggression, apathy, and fear. Developing the capacity to be able to say thank you for the lessons learned in good and bad times is a muscle that needs intentional attention. One way to develop the muscles of the attitude of gratitude is to say thank you for life and health today, for the wisdom that guides me, and for the gifts that allow me to help others.

Being able to see people as our equals will increase the ability to see their contributions to this world and the benefits we are receiving from their efforts. Imagine the ability to say thank you for the experiences of a painful encounter with a person or group that you gave permission to make you feel less than you are for generations or just a moment. Building the mental fortitude to say "thanks for what was learned and I value the internal and external beauty that I possess" is an incredible capability.

Ubuntu Creates Successful Organizations

An organization filled with the essence of Ubuntu is destined to win. One of the pillars of developing a strategy is identifying how to win. How powerful is it to know that your people already have what it takes to win? The quality of relationships with partners, peers, and leaders is built on the premise that we are equals and we are cheering for the success of all.

The behavior of most business leaders is to ensure that they get the best for themselves and squeeze business partners to receive less. The business leaders with the mental and emotional shift to treat partners as people and equals benefit from an improved relationship. The result is often improved value delivered in products and services and the willingness to go the extra mile to resolve issues as they are encountered. The only way to have Ubuntu as a value in your business is through the intentional act to lead by example and model the behavior for others to see. If done well, people may ask, "How do I have what our leaders have?"

Reflect, Relate, and Remember

The practice of Ubuntu is a transformative experience that brings out the best in our humanity. Perfection should not be expected, and we must realize that each man or woman must lean in to make a change. Begin by asking: To whom do you owe gratitude for helping you to be the amazing person you are? Who have you helped to see that they are your equal? What can you do to bring about small shifts in relationships with people who are not in your realm of influence?

BELONGING

I have discovered in life that there are ways of getting almost anywhere you want to go, if you really want to go.

– Langston Hughes

WHY IS BELONGING IMPORTANT?

"I long, as does every human being, to be at home wherever I find myself."
– Maya Angelou

We experience belonging when there is a sense of acceptance, inclusion, and identity within a specific group. Since birth, most humans have been guided to belong to our family and community. This behavior is not limited to humans but includes some mammals that are part of the animal kingdom. Harari (2015) describes belonging as "an intimate community where people know each other well and depend on each other for survival." *Homo sapiens* banded together to create a community for survival and protection. Being separated from the community could mean death physically and socially. Losing a sense of belonging creates anxiety that often leads to personal suffering that has generational impacts. Scanning the annals of history, there is evidence of groups of people who were denied acceptance and inclusion in communities across the world. The native people of the Americas were stripped of their birth land and limited to reservations and extinction. Africans were stolen from their native lands and made slaves in Europe, the West Indies, and the United States. People of the Jewish faith were imprisoned and killed in the Holocaust. These atrocities are the results of denying human beings a sense of belonging.

In work environments that allow the individual to bring their authentic self to work, there is a genuine sense of belonging. My experience with people from other countries, where they are allowed to share culture through food and celebrations, is a sense of genuine belonging. When people feel they belong at work, their performance and personal lives improve. Creating genuine experiences of belonging for all is of critical importance to improving engagement and performance within the business environment. The outcome helps support business goals.

Twaronite (2019) developed the EY Belonging Barometer study to uncover how more than 1,000 employed adult Americans define belonging. The respondents reported the following when asked in what ways they belong (Twaronite, 2019):

- 56% of respondents feel they belong most at work when they feel trusted and respected, with baby boomers feeling this way the most at 63%, compared with gen Xers at 56% and millennials at 53%.
- 39% of respondents feel they belong most at work when they can speak freely and voice their opinions.
- 34% feel they belong most at work when their unique contributions are valued, with Caucasian respondents agreeing the most at 36%, followed by black respondents at 31% and Hispanic respondents at 27%.

Many people spend fifty percent or more of their waking hours in the work environment five days a week. The amount of time spent at work is more than we spend with our family, at our place of worship, and in our community during the work week. This is another reason why belonging is so important. Expressing an appreciation for the unique backgrounds that each person brings in the workspace will improve the psychological and physical well-being of our colleagues.

Sharing the purpose (why) of belonging with everyone in the work environment creates compassion and transparency. Is there a way to use storytelling to share "why" belonging is critical for retaining people in an organization? One approach is to use an anonymous employee net promoter score (eNPS) to capture the sentiments of the people. The net promoter score (NPS) is a survey tool used by marketing professionals to learn about customers' loyalty to a brand. The primary question for the eNPS would be "Do you experience a sense of belonging in our organization?" The response options would use a simple Likert scale of strongly disagree, disagree, neither agree or disagree, agree, and strongly agree. The second question would be open ended, "Tell us what experiences informed your response."

The purpose (why) of the "belonging" message should not be limited to human resources (HR). Engaging all the people to share the positive and negative stories of belonging may improve acceptance, inclusion, and compassion. Ways to capture the voices of the many include belonging posters, open mic spoken word sessions, and/or open space events. The posters would share images and stories that highlight the purpose and benefits of each individual experience of belonging. The open mic spoken word sessions are the voices of people sharing their stories as an audio and/or video recording. The open space event is a small gathering where people announce a topic, people vote with their feet by going to a session or leaving it if they don't find value, and the outcome of the conversation is shared back with the community. Hosting a semi-annual or annual event for the festival of "belonging" would be an amazing experience for people to learn and share about each other.

Reflect, Relate, and Remember

Reflect on the purpose (why) belonging is important. What was memorable? What resonated? What are some ideas that you can relate to in this topic? What are the concepts that are most memorable for you? What could you do to push it further up the mountaintop? What's missing? What didn't work?

WHO NEEDS BELONGING?

Everyone needs belonging in a community or organization. Trevor Noah, the South African comedian and host of *The Daily Show,* struggled with belonging because of his bi-racial identity growing up in South Africa. In his book, *Born a Crime,* he shared about the struggles of finding belonging because of the laws in South Africa that could have landed him in an orphanage. A great deal of his childhood was spent in isolation because his grandparents were afraid the police could arrest them for associating with a child of bi-racial identity. In a recent interview on the CBS news show *60 Minutes,* Travor Noah said, "Everyone wants to belong. Half of our fights in life are because we want to belong", Stall (2022). The history of the white-body supremacy has been a continual devastation to people of color.

Belonging belongs to everyone in a work environment and community. One group of people does not hold a belonging monopoly over another group of people. The participation of all members of an organization is required to create a healthy space of working. Belonging helps to increase acceptance, inclusion, and compassion. Figure 1 illustrates the median belonging score from the survey results of college-educated professionals in May 2020.

***Figure 1**: Median belonging score by race and gender. **Adopted from**: Coqual (2020).*

The white men and women who ranked the highest in the belonging study in figure 1 are equally affected by the lack of belonging when they participate in excluding other groups in an organization or community. They must work extremely hard to do the wrong thing. Just imagine how much negative energy is stored up in one's mind, body, and spirit to maintain a deficit mindset. The deficit mindset is derived from deficit thinking, which is a pseudoscience founded on racial and class bias (Valencia, 1997).

Asian and black women have the lowest belonging scores in the workplace for college-educated professionals. White men and women have the highest belonging scores for college-educated professionals in the workplace. Black men and LatinX men and women are in the middle of the spectrum. Other groups that were not measured in figure 1 included lesbian, gay, bisexual, transgender and queer (LGBTQ+) people, people with neurodiversity, and people with mobility diversity needs.

People with neurodiversity, also referred to as neurodivergent, are individuals with brain processes that result in them learning and/or behaving differently from what is considered typical. Neurodivergent people may be diagnosed with autism, ADHD, OCD, dyspraxia, dyslexia, dyscalculia, or Tourette's Syndrome. Special accommodations may be required to activate their capabilities, such as headphones to prevent auditory overstimulation. The movie *Rain Man* illustrates some of the capabilities the character Raymond demonstrated with numbers. A powerful message that can be learned from the movie is the importance of understanding neurodiversity and how doing so can transform the perspective of a neurotypical individual and make them more empathetic in the process. We can learn from some of the key messages of the *Rain Man* movie as we prepare to practice belonging in our neurodiverse community. John Elder Robison stated, "Many individuals who embrace the concept of neurodiversity believe that people with differences do not need to be cured; they need help and accommodation instead."

People in need of mobility diversity have enjoyed policies in the United States through the Americans with Disabilities Act (ADA), which prohibits discrimination on the basis of disability in employment, state and local government, public accommodations, commercial facilities, transportation, and telecommunications. The ADA also applies to the United States Congress. A key issue at hand is how to deal with unconscious bias by individuals without disabilities. Unconscious bias, also known as implicit bias, is made up of social stereotypes about certain groups of people that individuals formed outside their own conscious awareness. Providing training to everyone in the organization to practice empathy and gain understanding of the challenges their colleagues may face will reduce the stigma of being disabled. Imagine the impact if everyone in the organization is aware of the tools and accommodations needed by someone with a disability. This would mean that anyone can play a supportive role in enabling a mobility diverse person to find belonging.

LGBTQ+ is a diverse group of people with their own language to talk about who they are and the challenges they face in society. Because of the diverse identities of this group of people, there will be a need to gain more knowledge about what is important to them. We have to be mindful not to put the burden of our own education on this group when there is a whole wide world of resources out there. We can begin by asking a powerful question like, *what is important to you*? The key is listening with empathy by seeking to understand what is important to the individual at the center of the conversation.

One of the primary lived LGBTQ+ stress points is hiding their true identity, often referred to as "being in the closet," out of fear for their safety. The lived experience is isolation, which robs the person of any feeling of belonging as well as any assistance in building resilience. Diamond (2013) explained, "The Minority Stress Theory specifies that sexual minorities' experience of acute exposure to environmental stressors such as verbal or physical abuse, institutional discrimination, interpersonal harassment, and general social marginalization, which confers cumulative psychological stress."

Love (patience and kindness) is one expression that can help foster belonging for everyone in an organization or community. The love expression described here is not the chemical reaction of feelings but an intentional behavior that is demonstrated through patience and kindness. First, show kindness by being accepting of the differences in people. Second, be patient with understanding what is unknown to your experience. Showing patience and kindness will go a long way to helping people feel a sense of belonging in your organization or community.

Imagine what would happen if all coworkers worked equally as hard in doing the right thing by allowing everyone to be included. Adopting an abundance mindset that believes there is enough capacity for everyone who wants to belong can contribute to helping the organization or community thrive. This includes resources, love, relationships, wealth, and opportunities. A phrase that I hear often from peers is health is the new wealth. Having a positive outlook on life ultimately leads to a reduction in stress, anger, fear, and increase in openness.

Reflect, Relate, and Remember

Who have you met lately who requires your expression of love (patience and kindness)? When have you encountered acts of discrimination in your life that you can connect with and relate back to showing kindness to others? What is coming up for you that will assist in remembering what powerful questions are important to ask?

THE LANGUAGE OF BELONGING

The adage of "sticks and stones can break my bones, but words can never harm me" is only partially true because words matter. Language is made of words, and words can be harmful to people in need of belonging. Verbal abuse is the use of words that are intended to diminish a person's well-being. Eleanor Roosevelt said, "No one can make you feel inferior without your consent." This quote is only true when you are in a place of mental and emotional strength. Words can definitely be harmful to your emotional and mental state, which in turn can be detrimental to your physical health. Words of affirmation are positive words and phrases used to uplift someone. The powerful words are helpful to uplift our spirit and make us feel kindness. A simple expression of "I value you because your partnership in our collaboration helps me with my blind spots" informs an individual of the value contributed in the partnership at work or home.

Language is very powerful and has the ability to unite or divide us. Sharing the same language builds camaraderie between individuals and supports a shared knowledge based on the words used. For example, when people say "break a leg," the intention is for someone to do well during a presentation or act. It is not intended for the individual to physically break a leg. It is common for people entering into a space where the language spoken is well known to experience belonging. The opposite is true when the language is foreign to you and causes you to feel that you don't belong. This is when someone can demonstrate courage by sharing the meaning of the language used in that community. We experience the invitation to learn something new, which gives us the ability to feel accepted.

The language of belonging is a tone of invitation, a voice of acceptance, and the sound of empathy. The tone of invitation says bring your whole self and you are welcome here. The voice of acceptance says that you are enough. The sound of empathy rings out that we are envisioning what it is like to be in your shoes. The language of belonging reverberates with joy and laughter in the core of the people receiving invitation, acceptance, and empathy.

The conversations begin with expressed gratitude, and we are open to explore areas that are sensitive and often restricted. Because we have an attitude of gratitude, we tread lightly and sometimes with a heavy footstep. But we have compassion for each other, and our self-awareness informs us on how our intent affects the people we encounter each day. Therefore, we show empathy to demonstrate that we will do everything humanly possible to understand where you are and have been. Figure 2 illustrates the importance of compassion that will help us reach beyond empathy.

EMPATHY BEYOND SYMPATHY

Figure 2: *Compassion goes beyond sympathy and empathy.* ***Adopted from:*** *Hougaard, R., Carter, J., and Marissa Afton, M. (2021).*

In our workplace, the shared language enables us to build a sustainable community that is welcoming. Grant (2021) said, "A workplace is a community—a place where people bond around shared values, feel valued as human beings, and have a voice in decisions that affect them." In the welcoming workplace, people experience reduced negative judgments because we have a bond around shared values. The shared values are the catalyst for establishing a generative culture. The original concept of the generative culture is performanced-based; however, it becomes more powerful when extended to include continual learning as a core practice. A continual learning organization is an agile organization that can inspect and adapt to challenges and opportunities. Learning helps people keep a broad perspective but focus on specific needs.

The language of racism and xenophobia does not holistically enable belonging. Instead, the racist and xenophobic words limit participation to the few people sharing this false sense of superiority. The people locked in the bubble of racism and xenophobia need empathy and compassion to grow into giving empathy and compassion to everyone.

The language of belonging helps us to demonstrate integrity with each other. This is accomplished by creating working agreements to hold each other accountable for the language used in our conversations.

Reflect, Relate, and Remember

What new language surfaced in your community that allowed you to feel a sense of belonging? Which words were relatable that gave you confidence to participate in the community? How will you remember what was learned?

SENSE YOUR SPACE FOR BELONGING

Belonging is essential to our human existence. Instinctually, our need to belong draws us into relationships that are helpful for spiritual, emotional, and physical development. The experience of healthy belonging in a positive relationship and environment helps us to feel valued. Some relationships may not always provide the beneficial experiences that we desire and can be deadly. Belonging can be a generative experience that is beneficial for everyone.

The "I Have a Dream" speech by Dr. Martin Luther King Jr., delivered on August 28, 1963, on the steps of the Lincoln Memorial in Washington DC, was a message of belonging.

Dr. King said:

> *When the architects of our republic wrote the magnificent words of the Constitution and the Declaration of Independence, they were signing a promissory note to which every American was to fall heir.*
>
> *This note was a promise that all men—yes, black men as well as white men—would be guaranteed the unalienable rights of life, liberty, and the pursuit of happiness.*

His words clearly stated that we all are heirs of belonging. All men and women—no matter their race, religious affiliation, gender preferences, or place of origin—are entitled to their space of belonging that includes life, liberty, and the pursuit of happiness.

Dr. King's message is still relevant today, especially in the current climate of political discourse and social injustice experienced in all corners of the world.

W. E. B. Du Bois wrote of the condition of double-consciousness that black people experienced in the United States in 1903. The double-consciousness represents two souls, two thoughts, two unreconciled strivings, and two warring ideals.

In present times, we call this code-switching. Code-switching is the conscious and unconscious behavior to act or talk more like those around you. In our space of belonging, we are free from double-consciousness and code-switching.

Start with the end in mind by defining where you would like to be and speaking into existence the place that fills you in all ways imaginable. Your selected space of belonging allows you to speak your truth in love. Psychological safety is well understood, and that is found where people are open to listening to ideas that are not part of the status quo without judgment. Sensing a safe space to experience belonging is an experiment. It will require careful attention to past experiences to determine what was generative and destructive.

I think of the times I would visit my mom's home on St. Croix in the United States Virgin Islands. The smell of a local meal bubbling on the stovetop in the kitchen and something yummy baking in the oven bring a delight to my senses. The roosters in the backyard would croon a melody that said, "Welcome, you belong here, remember!"

Those familiar moments are what resonate with me—where I can bring my complete self without a worry of bias and lack of opportunity. Even when I must share those moments with my siblings and other family members, the feeling of belonging is present and strong.

I forget how much of a privilege it was to grow up in a community where no one wanted to harm me because of my skin color. My skin color did not matter because the majority of the people in my community were black. My teachers, police officers, governors, shopkeepers, and people in most professions were black.

It is not to say that things were perfect. It was not Shangri-La. Some people practiced colorism and discriminated against other black people from other islands in the Caribbean. My family and friends all wanted me to be the best that I could be and belong. Growing up on St. Croix gave me a sense of belonging and confidence that I could do anything I put my mind to achieve. Every time I set my feet on that island rock, I feel like I belong, and that brings a sense of healing.

My son grew up in white-cultured Orange County, CA. He experienced the brunt of microaggressions and polite racism. He did not get the full benefit of belonging as I did. I hear my son's voice expressing that he does not know where he belongs.

"Am I black or Mexican? Am I Blaxican? Which culture should I lean toward? When I am with black people, I do not feel that I fit even though they can see that I have black features. When I am with Mexican people, my Spanish is limited, and I cannot relate to their experiences." My son did not have the luxury of being embedded in either culture, and now, he is seeking to find his place of belonging.

The ideal of a post-racial America fills us with misinformation that racism and limiting our sense of belonging is an experience of the past. The history is short, and we just need to look at the images of protests in 2020 because of violence and social injustice against people of color.

The January 6, 2021, insurrection is a recent historical event in which the safe transfer of power was challenged with violence, and our democracy could have been forever altered. These recent events contradict Dr. King's view of the Constitution as "a promissory note to which every American was to fall heir."

Rodney King famously asked, "Can we all just get along?"

Generative Workspace of Belonging

A generative belonging workspace is one where we are resilient in our ability to give birth to new ideals of who we are. We are allowed to bring our whole self to work and experiment to improve who we are. This space of belonging is for everyone in the organization to participate in. It is not limited to those marginalized by the behaviors and attitudes of the agents of discrimination and narcissism. The agents of discrimination and narcissism have a role in the learning and transformation to a generative workspace of belonging.

What if our work environment gave us a sense of belonging synonymous with hiking on a trail in a beautiful place? Recently, while hiking on the Fay Canyon Trail in Sedona, AZ, I had a sense of belonging with nature. The red rocks and green trees made it even more appealing to my senses. I wanted to be there while listening to the silence and the rustling of the tree leaves in the wind. The people walking along the trail were friendly, and we exchanged pleasantries of good morning and inquired about each other's well-being.

Is it possible for us to behave in this gentle way while trying to navigate a volatile, uncertain, complex, and ambiguous (VUCA) business environment by showing more patience and kindness (love) to each other? If we did, sensing our place of belonging would be much easier at work.

Don't Fake Belonging

Don't fake it 'til you make it! Many have tried this approach to no avail, and the results can be harmful to your mental health. Belonging is too important to your ability to thrive. So just don't do it. It is so easy to write that you shouldn't fake belonging. The reality is that you may be in situations that require the stance of faking it until you make it so that you may survive.

Realize that if you must fake it until you make it, limit the experience by creating a time-box. A much better approach is to be authentic, which signals that you are aware of yourself—that is the beginning of knowing where you belong and want to be. People enjoy authentic people and attach labels to describe their behaviors and aura. Those labels include, but are not limited to: maverick, fearless, honest, daring, and inspiring.

BACK 2 YOUR VISION PRACTICE

"Back 2 your vision" is a practice that was created to help people identify a vision during my professional coaching sessions. The goal is to create a vision that is a minimum of three months and no more than six months into the future, identify hurdles starting from the future (impediments) that you may encounter, and define the goals you want to achieve from the present to the future. Look at the Visioning Journey Map in Figure 3.

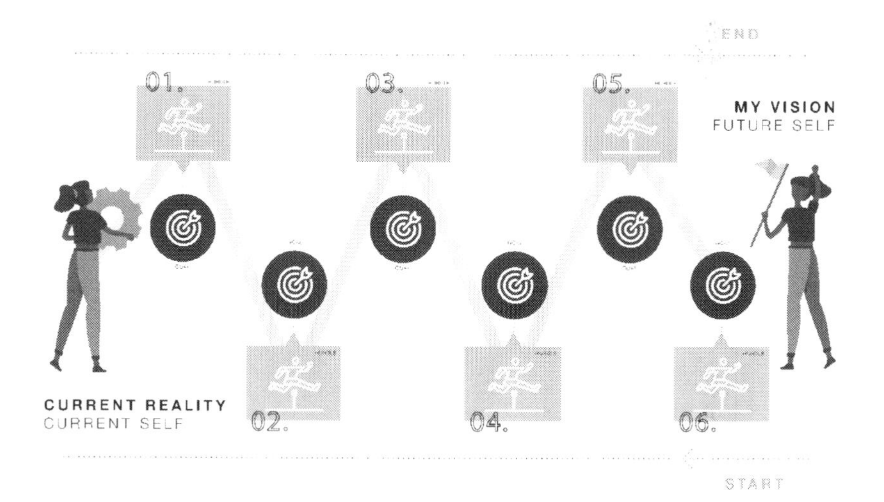

***Figure 3**: Visioning Journey Map.* ***Adopted from**: KnolShare.org*

When we develop a healthy sense of belonging, we can manage stress and anxiety more effectively, which results in a healthier and happy life. Buettner (2019) described the *blue zones* as destinations where people live to be 90 or more years old. Primary reasons for long life are having a sense of belonging in the community and eating a healthy diet. In short, I would suggest that belonging is self-love, self-respect, and self-care.

Use the Visioning Journey Map by following these instructions:

Step 1: Set your sights on a vision situated three to six months in the future.

Step 2: Start at the vision you chose three to six months down the road. These are depicted as "My Vision" and "Future Self" in Figure 3.

Step 3: Identify the hurdles that might limit your ability to reach this vision.

Step 4: Continue looking in reverse from the end of your journey, working until you reach "Current Reality" and "Current Self."

Step 5: Now that you have identified the hurdles you may encounter, begin your journey at the "Current Reality/Current Self" starting point in Figure 3.

Step 6: Start your journey by walking toward your future, acknowledging every one of the hurdles. Identify and capture those goals that line themselves up along the way.

Step 7: Make your vision more visible by hanging it and sharing what you discover along the way.

Reflect, Relate, and Remember

As you engage yourself with this activity, ask the following questions for a deeper connection:

- When facing each of the identified hurdles, who do you need to be?
- In what ways might seeing the world limit you?
- Who do you get to become when you have achieved the goals of the journey?
- What are the qualities required to make you feel satisfied along the way?
- Do you have the support system you might need as you continue the journey?
- Why is this vision significant to you?

When you are finished with the Visioning Journey, spend some time reflecting, relating, and remembering. Ponder these questions:

- What did you discover?
- Why were these selected hurdles important to you?
- How will you move forward with goals beyond that vision?

BELONGING STRATEGY

A belonging strategy will help a community or organization to create a vision that can be realized and changed when necessary. Strategy is a general direction set for a community, organization, or group to achieve a desired state in the future. Michael Porter (1996) said strategy is "deliberately choosing a different set of activities to deliver a unique mix of value." The definition of value is a measurable outcome that can be realized and shared. Strategy is the creation of a unique and valuable position and requires trade-offs in competing demands to choose what not to do. Strategy involves creating "fit" among a company's activities. Strategies should deliver a value that is beneficial to the people intended as the recipient of its goals.

The belonging strategy should be measurable, provide benefits to its intended recipients, achievable, and shareable. The approach to defining the belonging strategy will use the IDEO strategic process map defined in Figure 4.

STRATEGIC PROCESS
MAP

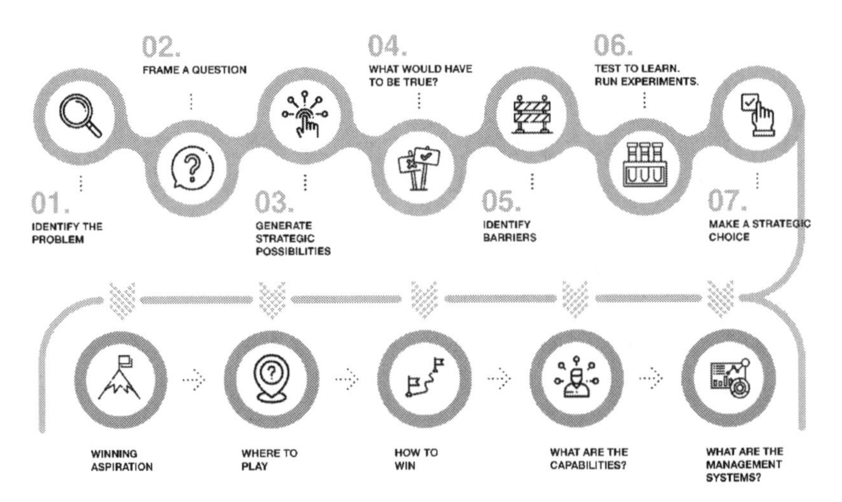

***Figure 4**: IDEO Strategic Process Map. **Adopted from**: IDEO U.*

The strategic process map provides seven steps to guide the approach when defining and evaluating one or more strategic themes. The journey of defining the belonging strategy requires building a team to ideate and generate strategic possibilities. The team should be diverse so that many viewpoints are heard and applied. The strategic process map playbook defines the following steps to develop a belonging strategy through a series of collaboration meetings:

Collaboration Meeting One:

Duration: 1 to 2 Days

Step one: Define the problem to focus the strategy work.

Step two: Frame a question with a prefix of "how might we."

Step three: Generate strategic possibilities (ideate to be specific, concrete, and actionable).

Between Collaboration Meetings:

Duration: 1 to 2 Weeks

Refine strategic possibilities: Refine to be specific, concrete, and actionable

Collaboration Meeting Two:

Duration: 1 to 2 Days

Step four: Ask what would have to be true to adapt to this strategic possibility.

Step five: Identify barriers for each strategic possibility (what is stopping the strategic choice?).

Step six: Test to learn for each strategic possibility (design and assign tests).

Between Collaboration Meetings:

Duration: 2 to 12 Weeks

Test to learn: Conduct tests and experiments

Collaboration Meeting Three:

Duration: 1 Day

Step seven: Make a choice by selecting one to three of the strategic possibilities.

The strategic process map playbook is a guide that can be customized to support each organization's needs. The goal is to activate the wisdom of the crowd to identify and deliver a unique mix of value for the belonging strategy that is vital for the organization to thrive in an increasingly diverse world. The belonging strategy should amplify all voices, clear barriers, and create space to appreciate each person for their unique backgrounds.

We will begin with unpacking the strategic problem: Organizations were designed to create belonging for only the patriarchal white male society. This strategic problem is large and is one thing blocking the organization from achieving success with "Belonging for All" as a winning aspiration. Step two of the strategic process map is to reframe the problem as a question. The primary question asked was "How might we get representation from white men and women, black men and women, Asian men and women, LatinX men and women, and allow neurodiversity, LGBTQ+, and mobile diversity to play a role in creating an environment of belonging for everyone?"

The recommendation will be to retain this monolith of a question but also create additional questions for each group. For example, "How might we enable belonging for LGBTQ+ members in our organization?" Creating specific questions for each group would provide the opportunity to go deeper with the next step of generating strategic possibilities that are specific, concrete, and actionable. A strategic possibility for the LGBTQ+ members in the organization is to not ask anyone to change their appearance to conform to company culture.

Step one - Define the problem: Organizations were designed to create belonging for only the patriarchal white male society.

Step two - Frame a question for the problem: How might we get representation from white men and women, black men and women, Asian men and women, LatinX men and women, and allow neurodiversity, LGBTQ+, and mobile diversity to play a role in creating an environment of belonging for everyone?

Step three - Generate strategic possibilities (be specific, concrete, and actionable): Your team collaborates to identify as many ideas as possible that are specific, concrete, and actionable. Capturing responses to the question of how we might get increased representation from a diverse community could be facilitated through an innovation session to capture the diverse voices and ideas. A virtual tool could be used by the facilitator to support individuals remotely and in the same location to place their ideas on a board for conversation and review.

Step four - What would have to be true: Discover what would have to be true to realize the strategic possibility. What would have to be true is if the organization has policies that allow its members to choose work attire with some guardrails. Some guardrails may include not wearing your birthday suit, beach outfits, or pajamas in the office.

Step five - Identify barriers: The organizing team identifies barriers that would make the strategic possibility unattainable or unsustainable. Some of the barriers may include people who are fearful that their privileged positions may decrease creating resistance to the change in being considered first for everything in the organization.

Step six - Test to learn, run experiments: Iterative prototypes are designed, implemented, and tested to have empirical results to increase knowledge and experience. Create small experiments that are ten to thirty days in duration to ask what is working and not working. The shorter feedback loops will help to verify our hypothesis about the validity of the experiments.

Step seven - Make a strategic choice: The organizing team comes to the inflection point to make a choice between the strategic possibilities that will be selected for implementation. The strategic decision is based on the strategy choice cascade illustrated in Figure 5. The five strategy choice cascade outputs include: 1) define the winning aspiration, 2) define where to play, 3) describe how to win, 4) identify the existing capabilities that need to be undertaken to build a sustainable opportunity, and 5) describe the infrastructure, systems, processes, and metrics that support and measure the strategy over time.

Figure 5*: Strategy choice cascade.* ***Adopted from****: IDEO U.*

The strategy choice cascade serves as the output of your strategy work to visualize and share your strategy with others. The winning aspiration describes what to accomplish together and builds alignment with the organization members. Where to play identifies the location, people, and product/service offering that potential customers will experience. How to win is the competitive advantage that describes the differentiators that will be realized by the strategy possibilities. The capabilities are the activities needed to build the competitive advantages to win. The management systems include technology platforms, organizational structures, training programs, and key measures.

Adaptive System of Belonging

Finding companies that emphasize a culture of belonging, where the culture welcomes you to co-create spaces for healthy conversation about our shared humanity, is rare. The future of work may push organizations to develop a bridge toward greater empathy and inclusion. Kennedy and Jain-Link (2021) developed a quantifiable definition that stated we belong at work when we are:

- *Seen* for our unique contributions
- *Connected* to our coworkers
- *Supported* in our daily work and career development
- *Proud* of our organization's values and purpose

Reflect, Relate, and Remember

Think about how you would form a team to support defining the belonging strategy. This work is best achieved with a team of passionate people. When thinking about the belonging strategy, did anything surprise or inspire you to think differently about how you understand defining a belonging strategy's choices or strategic problem? Is there something that you hope to remember as you try to articulate your own strategy problem and apply the "how might we" question?

IMPLEMENTING THE BELONGING STRATEGY

Implementing the belonging strategy is an organizational change management (OCM) initiative. OCM is about people and the ability of individuals to shift behaviors to align with the proposed change. OCM helps to identify who's impacted by a change and ensure they are knowledgeable about and supportive of the change efforts. The belonging strategy will require awareness fostered by effective communications, knowledge on how to change, and the reinforcements necessary to sustain change. As described in the belonging strategy chapter, working as a team will yield the best results for implementing the belonging strategy.

The strategic possibility question previously identified was "How might we get representation from white men and women, black men and women, Asian men and women, LatinX men and women, and allow neurodiversity, LGBTQ+, and mobile diversity to play a role in creating an environment of belonging for everyone?" Implementing a strategy of this size will require a structured approach to implementing the belonging strategy that will serve the team by providing clear guidelines for implementing the change. To implement the belonging strategy, the Kotter 8-step change management process will be used to help lead the change. Figure 6 illustrates the eight steps to support a sustainable belonging strategy.

The eight steps are:

1. create a sense of urgency
2. build a guiding coalition

3. form a strategic vision and initiatives
4. enlist a volunteer army
5. enable action by removing barriers
6. generate short-term wins
7. sustain acceleration
8. institute change

THE BIG **OPPORTUNITY**

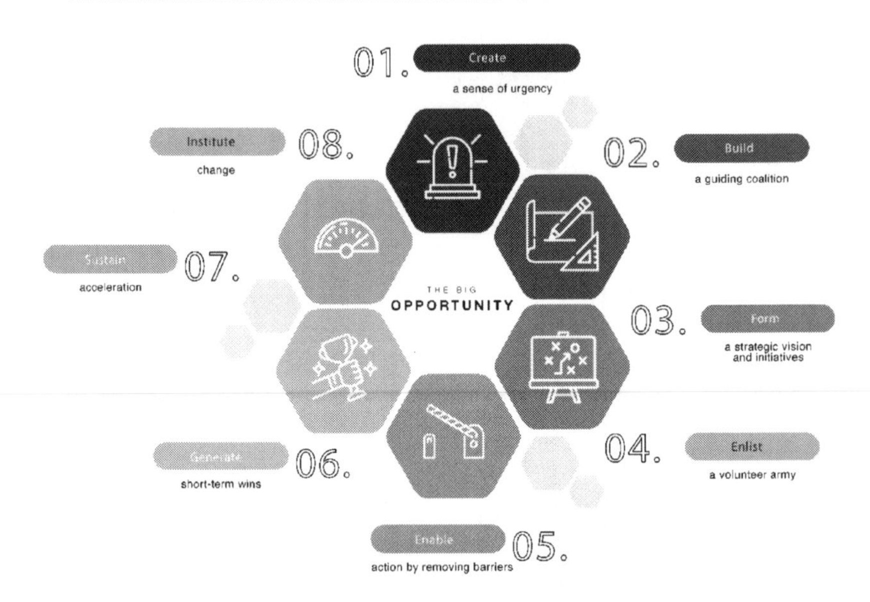

***Figure 6**: Kotter 8-Step Change Management. **Adopted from**: Kotter, J.A. (2014). Accelerate (XLR8): Building strategic agility for a faster-moving world.*

Go deeper by asking transformative questions to gain more insights into why change is important. Figure 7 describes the Kotter 8-step change process evaluation inquiry to identify the purpose for change and increase the urgency and awareness for the change.

Step 1: Create a sense of urgency. Ask the question, why is this important now?

Step 2: Build a guiding or transformational coalition. Inquire who you will partner with for success.

Step 3: Form a strategic vision and initiatives. Ponder how we align on a common vision.

Step 4: Enlist a volunteer army. Probe what story we tell our people.

Step 5: Enable action by removing barriers. Evaluate what will stop or slow progress toward the goals.

Step 6: Generate short-term wins. Encourage the exploration of what incremental experiments are possible to validate the goals. Additionally, we would want to use telemetry to discover how we know that progress is made toward the goals.

Step 7: Sustain acceleration. Encourage inquiry in how we can avoid slow victories. Step 8: Institute change. Seek how we can anchor sustainable change in our culture.

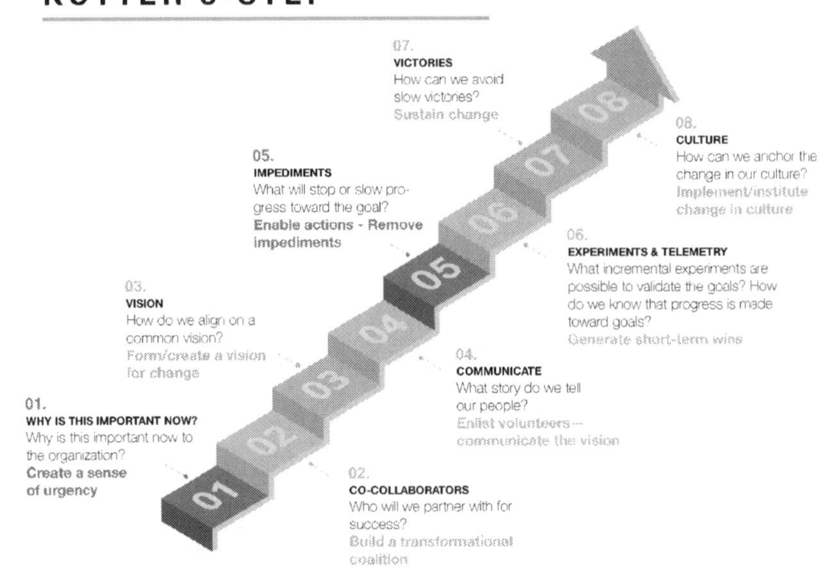

***Figure 7**: Evaluate change with Kotter 8-Step.* ***Adopted from**:* *Kotter, J.A. (2014). Accelerate (XLR8): Building strategic agility for a faster-moving world.*

The OCM approach will provide insights into the challenges and opportunities that may occur during the belonging strategy implementation. The guiding principles for the belonging strategy should include: 1) design for human connection, 2) respect for people and culture, and 3) make it equitable. Designing for human connection begins with people at the center of the discussion. The design for human connection includes physical space that supports easy connection through shared spaces to break bread and have conversations. The respect for people and culture guiding principle ensures that we consider the beliefs, values, and norms that matter most to people.

Culture will be a major contributor for people likely to resist the belonging strategy change. However, with a well-designed

OCM approach, a plan can be created to get the resisters to participate so their voices can be heard. The belonging strategy implementation must be equitable to account for everyone in the organization's community. Countless research and evidence is widely available demonstrating the marginalization of white women, black men and women, Asian men and women, LatinX men and women, and neurodiversity, LGBTQ+, and mobile diversity individuals. We have to show grace and inclusion to those afflicting the trauma so they can find redemption in their journey of belonging. This is a critical step in the process of creating space for belonging that belongs to everyone.

Reflect, Relate, and Remember

Implementing the belonging strategy is about changing how people connect with each other to co-create a community for everyone to experience belonging. OCM is a systemic way for planning change in any system, which includes organizations and communities. In the journey of implementing the belonging strategy, consider the following: How can you create awareness? What actions will be taken to increase knowledge that enables people to change? How will you assemble a team of co-collaborators to sustain change for everyone to experience belonging?

HEALING

Healing happens when you move through the pains, the patterns, and stories, and walk your way to a healthy ending.

– Vienna Pharaon

Forgive yourself for not knowing what you didn't know before you learned it.

– Maya Angelou

THE ROOT BEFORE THE FRUIT

Healing is a slow process, and it takes time for us to metabolize the experiences that affected us physically, spiritually, and mentally. The healing journey is oftentimes a response to trauma, which is the negative experiences that others afflict us with. When it is afflicted by others, trauma is those experiences that happen to us without our permission. We can also be perpetrators of trauma on ourselves and others.

The root before the fruit concept describes the need for solid roots to support a sustainable opportunity to bear fruit in our healing space. The parable of the sower from the Bible describes how healing may occur in our lives by describing the seed and the soil that creates a home for the seed to take root and grow into a fruit-bearing and life-giving tree. Our mind, body, and spirit are represented by the soil, and the healing is the seed that is planted in us to help move forward in the journey of healing. Matthew 13:3-8 says, "'A farmer went out to sow his seed. As he was scattering the seed, some fell along the path, and the birds came and ate it up. Some fell on rocky places, where it did not have much soil. It sprang up quickly, because the soil was shallow. But when the sun came up, the plants were scorched, and they withered because they had no root. Other seed fell among thorns, which grew up and choked the plants. Still other seed fell on good soil, where it produced a crop—a hundred, sixty or thirty times what was sown.'"

Sowers want good soil to plant seeds. Good soil is rich with nutrients, which create a place for plants to have an abundant food supply to support healthy development. Good seeds are also essential for the process of growing healthy fruits. Quality seeds contain high protein, starch, and oil reserves that help in the early stages of growth and development. The healing (seed) and our mind, body, and spirit (soil) must equally be of good quality. The mind, body, and spirit may start out in a state that needs improvement, but with time, they will become resilient to produce a multiplier effect of the healing received.

The healing remedies may be experienced differently based on how each person is able to metabolize the seed(s) in the mind, body, and spirit. The mind may respond to psychotherapy and coaching. The body may excel with somatic healing and exercise to create endorphins that are beneficial. The spirit may soar with meditation and organized spirituality to help create focus for the healing to be sustainable. Each person's experience may be different, and in some cases, it may not work at all. When the healing is not beneficial, seek the opportunity to explore and experiment with other options. We must be persistent in finding a path forward to dampen the trauma and amplify the healing experience.

Not everyone will be able to lay down roots to produce the fruit of healing. This reality is hard to accept, but as a professional coach, I must remove my biases and ego to allow someone more equipped with the appropriate knowledge and skills to support the client in pursuing healing. In my experience as a professional coach, I have been in situations where I was unable to guide a client to develop the roots necessary for healing because the subject was something that required a psychotherapist. There is no harm in asking if it is okay to provide a referral for a traumatic topic that is beyond your scope of knowledge. The client's healing is most important.

Experiencing healing in a community setting is extraordinarily powerful and provides the opportunity to receive as well as to give in the journey of developing the root before the fruit. In some communities, the healing experience may include the mind, body, and spirit. This is beneficial to provide a consistent context for the healing experience. A federated community healing experience for the mind, body, and spirit may also be beneficial. The diversity of the healers may bring a fresh context that increases the effectiveness in the mind, body, and spirit because each healer is specialized in a specific discipline. The individuals receiving the healing will have to reconcile how each healing experience relates to the others. The question that may arise is how do organized spirituality, meditation, and yoga complement each other? We know that organized spirituality uses prayer, which can be viewed as a focused meditation with a supreme being at the center of healing. Meditation is used in yoga to support the calming of the mind and body. Yoga can connect the mind, body, and spirit in a single experience.

The root before the fruit is core to experiencing a sustainable mind, body, and spirit healing effect. When there is no root, the healing will not stick and the individual can become discouraged because of the failure. The path to having roots to bear fruit takes practice and persistence. Michael (Air) Jordan, the basketball legend, said, "I've missed more than nine thousand shots in my career. I've lost almost three hundred games. Twenty-six times I've been trusted to take the game-winning shot and missed. I've failed over and over and over again in my life." What would have happened if Air Jordan had decided that taking the twenty-seventh game-winning shot was too much to bear in failure?

What would have happened if the men and women fighting for civil rights decided that the dog bites, jail time, and physical beatings were too much to withstand in Alabama, Mississippi, Georgia, and other places in the United States? A great amount of anxiety rises in me as I dare to invite those thoughts in my mind.

I would like to state again: the healing (seed) and our mind, body, and spirit (soil) must equally be of good quality. The mind, body, and spirit will become resilient to produce a multiplier effect of the healing received.

Reflect, Relate, and Remember

The healing journey is not simple and requires trial and error over time. Oftentimes, there will be twists and turns as the journey zig zags to deliver us on a path of healing. The intentional effort is what helps to develop the deep roots so there can be an abundance of fruits produced in healing.

When you think of healing, what comes to mind for you? What actions will be taken to develop a consistent habit to build the roots before the fruits? How can you develop a portrait of resilience as you walk toward healing?

HEALING IS THE ANTIDOTE TO TRAUMA

It is important to traverse the transformative journey of trauma to realize healing. Trauma is experienced physically, mentally, and spiritually. Trauma is a source of pain that we can describe and give a name. In my experience of the journey, I traveled back in time to my senior year in high school. Number 7, point guard, four year varsity starter, meet my alter-ego Mystic. I started as a freshman at St. Joseph High School and then three years at Central High School on the island of St. Croix USVI. The irony was that Central was playing St. Joseph, my former school, and we (Central) were killing them with the full-court press. I was the tip of the spear during the full-court press, and during one play, I dislocated my right knee. The adrenaline was pumping at such a high level that I slipped it back in place and continued playing for a few more plays.

Suddenly, pain began to throb like I have never experienced before. I signaled to my coach Danny Cornelius that I needed a substitute so I could come out of the game. He said, "I need to have you run more laps during practice because you never want a sub." I said, "Coach, my knee is killing me!" By the end of the first half, my knee was swollen to the size of a large grapefruit. At the end of the game, my teammates helped me into the back of Coach Cornelius's truck and drove me home. On the way home in the back of the truck, I placed a towel over my head and cried like a baby.

I said to myself that my dream and fantasy of playing for a Division-I college was over. To add further insult to injury,

I could not walk up the stairs to enter the second level of my home. Coach Cornelius picked me up like a baby and carried me up the stairs. Coach Cornelius was six feet nine inches tall and was a former starting center for St. John University in Queens, New York. This was one of my first major trauma experiences that required me to traverse the transformative journey of trauma to realize healing.

The context that I will use to categorize the transformative journey of trauma to realize healing is generative healing and limiting healing. Generative healing is the transformative journey that gives new opportunities to produce a favorable outcome. The days spent running in the ocean made me feel weightless, which made it possible to put some pressure on my right foot without much pain, and that experience gave the feeling that healing was in progress. The physical movement in the ocean was a somatic healing experience that helped with repairs on a cellular level in the body. Movement is healing, and the ability to engage in physical exercise allowed me to not dwell on the traumatic experience of injuring my knee.

Limiting healing creates a state of mind and conviction that the pain is too pervasive and healing is not possible. The days spent with healer Johnny Belardo were not for the faint at heart. He would give me sugar cane stems to chew on, while sitting in a chair with my right leg on his thigh. From a transparent glass bottle, he poured out a handful of oil and began massaging the quadricep muscles above my knee, which were very tense. He would pass my knee and begin massaging the calf muscles below the knee. Finally, the moment of truth came and he used both hands to massage the injured knee, and that sent needles up and down the right leg.

The first experience with Johnny Belardo created a moment of fright, freeze, and the desire for flight. My body responded to the knee massage with a recoil of my foot, which knocked the bottle of healing oil on the ground. Johnny shouted, "If you want to be healed, you have to sit still in the pain of healing." My mental state was that this was too much to bear, and I would often ask him to stop with tears running down my face because of the intense pain. This felt useless and my knee would never heal enough so that I could get back to playing basketball or just running, for that matter. I was definitely in the limiting healing space.

The Healing Power of Forgiveness

Forgiveness is a powerful state of spiritual, mental, and physical presence that allows each person to move beyond the trauma experienced. Forgiveness is a gift that is created through the experience of Ubuntu, the power of seeing each person as a person. Ubuntu is a human quality that includes the essential human virtues of compassion and humanity. Forgiving the perpetrator of trauma is hard because it requires courage and empathy. Courage is needed to confront the person, trauma, and fear to begin the journey of moving forward to a safe space where a name and description can be attached to the traumatic experience. Children abandoned by their birth parents have the fortitude to say, "I forgive you in spite of you abandoning me when I was helpless."

You may not be able to physically engage the person who caused the trauma because they may have moved on from this physical space on earth. You may not be able to confront the trauma perpetrator because being in the same space may trigger the trauma experience again and limit the opportunity for healing.

Empathy provides the ability to see the trauma perpetrator's context that may allow the gift of forgiveness. Having empathy for the trauma perpetrator does not mean you have to accept their behavior or beliefs. It may provide a window to see the limitations that they have and help you to understand the cause of their behavior and beliefs.

Forgiveness is a journey, and sometimes it may cause you to walk several steps toward a place of feeling safe and emotionally free. The steps in the journey may include:

1. Acknowledging the trauma experienced by giving it a name.
2. Identifying who hurt you and how much time passed since the experience.
3. Considering how the trauma changed you.
4. Accepting that you cannot change the past.
5. Learning what forgiveness means to you.
6. Determining whether or not you will offer forgiveness to begin or end the forgiveness journey.
7. Working on the forgiveness journey.
8. Forgiving the person who wronged you. This can be silent without engaging with the person who wronged you.
9. Releasing yourself from the emotional prison.
10. Practicing love by showing kindness and patience with yourself and the person who wronged you.

The journey of forgiveness will release many negative energies stored in your body and mind so that positive energies can emerge. Imagine using the new positive energy as a creative source to do things that you could not before. The positive creative source may open opportunities for healthy and sustainable relationships.

Forgiveness is not easy because it is often more comfortable to remain in the trauma experience where it can feel most familiar. The lack of forgiveness can be similar to having the state of mind of holding a grudge against someone, which is like drinking poison and then hoping the other person dies. The experience of participating in the TRC at the end of apartheid in South Africa must have been difficult for the people afflicted with trauma. As someone living a few countries afar, it was difficult for me to hear the stories of human rights abuses and be able to see forgiveness as a way to healing. The TRC was the method chosen by Archbishop Desmond Tutu and President Nelson Mandela to bring about unity in their country by practicing Ubuntu.

What lessons can be learned from the practice of Ubuntu during the TRC? Clearly, forgiveness leads the way for mothers, fathers, brothers, sisters, and other family members to give the gift of forgiveness to the trauma perpetrators. The trauma perpetrators had to publicly tell their stories of participating in the human rights abuses that led to loss of life and freedom. Unlike the Nuremberg trials in Germany, most of the trauma perpetrators received forgiveness for the crimes committed against the people of South Africa. The goal was restorative justice versus retributive justice.

Somatic Healing

A common practice for companies before the COVID-19 pandemic was to bring physical activities onto the corporate campus. The activities may include a gym, yoga classes, massage sessions, and high-intensity interval training (HIIT) for people to opt in to as participants. Somatic healing experiences engage the body and draw from the basic functions of the nervous system in treatment. Somatic therapy operates off the idea that what happens to you in your life is stored not only in your mind but also in your body. By focusing on both the physical sensations in your body and the discussion of your problems, it is a comprehensive approach to therapy.

Somatic healing has been beneficial after experiencing microaggression at work and in my dwelling community. Getting the frequent message that I am so intelligent and a credit to my race feels condescending, especially when I do not hear the same message being shared with my white male peers. Engaging in a yoga pose immediately after the microaggression often helps to release the negative energy from my body and mind. A few deep breaths allows my mind to consider an appropriate response so that I can experience frequent healing moments and not have a stiff knot in my neck or shoulders because I was too passive.

Psychotherapy Healing

Psychotherapy, also known as talk therapy, is a healing method to help people become whole by working with a trained therapist through deep conversations and inquiry. Some of the common uses of talk therapy include: anger management, grief, anxiety, phobias, and other mental health conditions. Many of these conditions are caused by traumas resident in people's environments and experiences. In the COVID-19 experience, tele-therapy is available to connect to trained therapists that meet people's time availability and options. The need to drive to an office to sit on a couch or chair for treatment is replaced by the opportunity to be treated in the convenience of your home or on a walk in the park. Support groups provide another talk therapy avenue that can be beneficial through listening and learning from other people's experiences.

Professional Coaching

Business, executive, and organizational coaching is focused on helping the individual or group to achieve future goals and resolve current conditions that are affecting progress. Coaching emphasizes getting the individual or group to realize their desired destination. The belief in coaching is that each person is whole and capable of finding a desired solution through exploration and discovery with a coach or on their own. When a coach observes certain mental health conditions that are beyond the scope of professional coaching, a referral can be offered to help the individual find appropriate alternative healing options.

Professional coaching is useful for organizations, employees, and individuals. The practice does not dwell on the past but seeks to help the individual or group to move forward toward a solution that satisfies the challenges or trauma that needs relief. Coaching in business settings enables employees to build the skills, mindsets, and behaviors needed to perform at their peak, both personally and professionally. The emphasis on coaching the person or group creates the opportunity to build the whole person and whole group. If a person is angry because their voice was silenced during meetings, the coach creates space for thought partnership that supports the person to have a conversation about what they experienced, create a plan to make their voice heard, and hold them accountable to their plan. The coach is not the owner of the plan, actions, or desired outcome. The coaching relationship builds individual or group resilience to help people thrive. Resilient people build resilient teams, and resilient teams transform a company to be high performing and sustainable.

My work as a business, executive, and enterprise organizational coach focuses on belonging and healing to support my clients' goals. The mantra that I speak into my client relationships is "helping people to achieve their level of awesomeness." The reward of being a thought partner and observing a client moving forward from the stronghold of anxiety, racism, sexism, bullying, or microaggression creates generative healing in the space that I hold as a coach.

A recent coaching session enabled a client to find a path forward to realize the amount of control and power that was in her hands. The African American female executive felt that she was not being heard by another white male executive and was on the verge of expressing frustration publicly. The good news is she brought the frustration and anxiety to a coaching session and we were able to navigate the source of frustration, identify her available personal power, and create a plan that can be realized and measured. In a twenty-five-minute coaching session, the female executive found her power and truth to thrive in a white-male-dominant technology environment. The power of professional coaching is helping people to use the incredible amount of resources already resident within them.

Spiritual Healing

Spiritual healing may consist of meditation, prayer, touching with healing intent, or communication with the spirit realm to facilitate self-healing or divine-healing in the individual or group. Meditation sessions are offered at some organizations to create space to explore thoughts and feelings within the individual headspace. The experience can free the mind and spirit to perform at an elevated level during the work day. Mindfulness meditation has proven to help reduce stress and anxiety and reduce blood pressure. The focus in the present moment minimizes the chance of making mistakes and improves cognitive function. Meditation can be done through a tele-health application at home or any location with a mobile device connection. Several organizations provided subscriptions to employees to engage in meditation while working at home during the COVID-19 pandemic.

Communicating with the divine creator through prayer is a powerful way to have a conversation about gratitude through the good and bad times. Living a life of gratitude creates a perspective that each day of life is a gift, no matter the challenges that are present in your life. An attitude of gratitude is the space that I try to walk in each day. There are days when an attitude of gratitude can be difficult to speak into existence, much less live. Each day, I start with uttering, "Thank you for life and the abundance that I am given today. Help me to use the gifts given to help others and myself to reflect goodness in this world." Speaking the words of gratitude out loud is helpful as it fills the rooms in your home, mind, body, and spirit with the sound of what is possible today.

Reflect, Relate, and Remember

Healing is a journey that most people would like to come easily. Some people pray for healing without investing the time and energy required to receive the outcome of being whole. Faith without works does not yield fruit. The mind, body, and spirit must traverse the transformative journey of trauma to realize healing. Generative and limiting healing is relevant in our physical, mental, and spiritual agency. Each healing experience brings us closer or further away from the desired outcome of releasing the pain of trauma.

As you meditate on healing in your life, ponder the questions that follow. How has generative healing played a role in repairing a physical trauma? When was limiting healing a barrier to achieving lasting healing? Where is spiritual healing in your journey?

EPILOGUE

This book concludes with conversations between Dr. Dave Cornelius, Tracy Treacy from D & S Healing Center, and Nobantu Mpotulo from Ubuntu Coaching posted on the *KnolShare with Dr. Dave* podcast. We want to share conversations about several topics in the book that include perspectives not captured in the formal writing. The conversations are impromptu and may contain some language that people may find offensive. Belonging is messy and requires significant efforts to ensure belonging belongs to everyone. Healing is not straightforward, and we must endure generative and limiting healing to traverse the transformative journey toward healing.

BELONG AND HEALING - UBUNTU: A CONVERSATION WITH DR. DAVE AND NOBANTU MPOTULO

Podcast: *KnolShare with Dr. Dave,* found on Spotify, iTunes, Audible, and Google Play

VLog: https://vimeo.com/694573342

Dr. Dave:

Hello, and welcome to the *KnolShare with Dr. Dave* podcast. This is Dr. Dave Cornelius, your host. And my conversation today is with Nobantu Mpotulo from Ubuntu Coaching. And our conversation will cover the practice of Ubuntu and see how that could play a really important role in belonging and healing in organizations and community. So Nobantu, why don't you share a little bit about who you are with our audience? And hopefully I'm saying your name correctly.

Nobantu:

Nobantu, yes.

Dr. Dave:

Nobantu, yes.

Nobantu:

Thank you very much. Yes. A very important name for me indeed. And *Bantu* in my language, which is Xhosa, means "people." So *Nobantu* means "mother of the people." And I find that in our culture, we name our children with the hope that the name would be fulfilled. And I found that I followed the helping professions, starting off as a psychologist, and I worked at institutions of higher learning as a student counselor and also counseling staff. And from there, I branched into coaching executives in organizations, and also, I'm a facilitator of peace circles, and Ubuntu plays a very critical and central role in my work.

Dr. Dave:
That's so great. So you are an accredited master certified coach at MCC from the International Coaching Federation. So how do you define Ubuntu?

Nobantu:
Ubuntu is the way of being, way of life that takes into cognizance the importance of interconnection, the importance of working with others, the importance of seeing the good in others. So if we define Ubuntu in my language isiXhosa, ais Umntu Ngumntu Ngabantu. I am because we are. I cannot be fully myself if you are not fully who you are destined to be. So in essence, what this is saying is that whatever I do, I can be more with others involved. And we have a proverb in Africa that says if you want to work fast, go together. Go alone, sorry. If you want to go far, go together. Let me say that again. If you want to go far, go together. If you want to go fast, go alone. So the spirit of Ubuntu is a spirit of moving from I-centrism to we-centrism.

Dr. Dave:
So if Ubuntu is the spirit of being focused on we, what are the benefits to a person, to an organization if they practice Ubuntu?

Nobantu:
If, for instance, we take diversity, inclusion, and belonging, we cannot be an organization that is successful or that is able to get far if, for instance, we focus on the competencies, on the

strengths, on the resources of individuals. But if we take all of those collectively and looking at our bigger goal, looking at our global goal objective that we want to reach, then with all those different competencies, different ways of how people are, we [are] able to enrich this objective we want to achieve. And as I'm saying that, I'm thinking of Maya Angelou's saying where she said that if you look at a tapestry on the wall, it's not the individual colors, the individual shapes of that tapestry that make it to be beautiful, but it's all of those combined together. And if you take one of those, then that tapestry becomes something else. So in diversity, in interconnectedness, in inter-beingness, there is more value, there is more beauty, there is more sustainability in what we want to achieve.

Dr. Dave:
So if we are working in a disconnected organization, how would Ubuntu help people build bridges?

Nobantu:
I want to answer this with a story because we're storytellers in Africa. There's a tribe in Zambia, the Bemba tribe. And what this tribe does, for instance, if someone is, I would say, menace in the society, they are a troublemaker, instead of casting that person out, what this tribe in the spirit of Ubuntu does, they as a community, as the village, get together—the young and the old, all generations—they form a circle, they get this person in the middle of the center, and then instead of chastising the person and pointing out the bad deeds, they focus on all good qualities of this person and point out those good qualities, the strengths and how these strengths impact the society and the community positively.

And as they do that, then the person also sees the goodness in themselves that is recognized by the others. And it's amazing how much this has a positive impact. And then after that, there's a celebration. There's a feast to celebrate this person. And this person recognizes that they are valued, they are seen. Because at times, people become a bad player in a team, the weak link. Not only because they are a bad person, maybe because there's something they need. And if you look at the nonviolent communication approach, it's exactly that as we notice what doesn't fit the values of the whole. Instead of just casting out the one who is not subscribing to those values, can we, in the spirit of Ubuntu, look at what does this person need? Can we come from a compassionate stance? And it's amazing how much when we do that, the person feels they have been included. And we as the collective continue to do the work in a collective manner.

Dr. Dave:
Very powerful, very powerful with that story. So as we take that story and we start looking at an organization working to experience belonging and healing, how would they benefit from Ubuntu?

Nobantu:
It's exactly like ... Think about an organization: what kills organizations is working in silos. What kills organizations is unhealthy competition. What kills organizations is also the form of rewards that we have which are somehow focused on rewarding individuals. So I have to get everyone out of my way to get to the top. So if you're thinking about Ubuntu, let's take the reward system. Instead of just focusing on rewarding and recognizing individuals, we can start looking at recognizing and rewarding teams.

And as we do that, we find that much distance could be covered by teams rather than individuals. Because if we focus too much on individuals, then we would find this individual who is so driven, who even in the end ends up being burnt out. Because singularly all they're thinking about is that I want to get that award today or this year again and be that best employee of the year. How does it become if we start to look at the best team and to ... With Ubuntu, if you look at it, it also promotes the collaboration between teams. And as we do that, everyone feels part of the organization, everyone buys into the overall, the global goal, the global destination we [are] going to. And as such, they become part of that.

Dr. Dave:
I could so relate to, in the earlier parts of my career, that desire to go fast, the desire to go alone and climb to the top. So as you were speaking, that really resonates with me personally. So I think of, like, what reflection of ourselves would we see when Ubuntu is present?

Nobantu:
I'm thinking right now as I'm thinking about this because I'm a visual person. I'm thinking about when there's a race and you look at the athletes, everyone is looking forward. On your marks, get set, go. And I always get amazed at how no one in that line looks back and thinks about the others who [are] coming, hey. It's like, "All I'm thinking is the finish line, and I want to be number one." And I always wonder, how would it be if as we are about to take this race, on your marks, get set, look back, who can you take along? And how would it be to win together?

And as I am with this, I'm thinking about a story of a researcher who came to Africa, an anthropologist. And this anthropologist saw a group of kids playing in this village that didn't have a lot of resources. And what he did, he had a bag of sweets, and he took this bag and put it under a tree and said to the kids, "Okay, race each other, and whoever gets to the bag of sweets, all those sweets are the winner's sweets." And so the kids ran and the researcher was amazed. The first one who got the bag, instead of taking the spoils for himself, this boy took the sweets and shared the sweets with the others. So what I'm trying to say here, when we practice Ubuntu, whether at home, in communities, in organizations, we all become winners.

Dr. Dave:
So powerful, so powerful when we all are winners and not just single out one person in an organization or community. So what does it mean when it's said that someone has Ubuntu?

Nobantu:
Someone with Ubuntu is a person, to me, who is in touch with his or her heart, someone who recognizes the suffering of the world, the suffering of others, and not just have empathy, but moves to compassion and takes action. And also it's someone on the other side who recognizes the joys and the successes of others and celebrates these successes and joys with the others. So this is a person who sees good in others. And when others are down and out, this is the person who's there to give a helping hand. That's a person with Ubuntu. And Ubuntu doesn't mean that that person could be a walkover, could be a doormat. For me, real Ubuntu comes with courage. If I love you, I see myself in you. I should be able to give you constructive feedback when you are doing injustice to yourself, when you are not fully becoming who you [are] destined to be because of the deeds that you engaged in. So it's both the heart, it's both the backbone and the knowing that all those who came before us, our ancestors, are always there; they always have our back.

Dr. Dave:
Yeah, that's so good. I really enjoyed that, what you just said about that. So when we think of someone, and this is the last question, how can someone elevate their sense of gratitude through the practice of Ubuntu?

Nobantu:
I would say Ubuntu is about authenticity; it's not a staged act. And I believe that a true sense of gratitude emerges when we do good deeds without expecting reward, when these good deeds come because I want to help. And as such, I do not attach to outcomes about I've helped you, then you should be eternally be grateful to me or indebted to me. I'm doing this because I'm seeing myself in you, and as I am doing this to lift another person, I'm lifting myself up. So with that, gratitude becomes organic and the heart expands, the heart opens. And if you think about neuroscience, what research says, a grateful and open and a compassionate heart leads to wellness, especially to mental wellness. So Ubuntu should not be performed to receive gratitude from others, but it's kind of, Ubuntu and gratitude, it's kind of two wings of the same bird.

Dr. Dave:
So I love the fact that we're talking about [how] an open and compassionate heart leads to wellness. And to me, that is such an important aspect in our lives, of how we could connect with other people. So we could have that sense of gratitude just to know that we know you and you know me and we could know each other based on our relationships. Is there anything finally you would like to share about Ubuntu before we close out our conversation here today?

Nobantu:
I would say it's an encouragement to fellow humans to see what everyday deeds they can include in their lives that are geared towards Ubuntu, seeing the other. When we greet in isiZulu, we say Sawubona, meaning I see you. As you go about your day, are you able to see others? Are you able to see the cashier at the supermarket? Just saying a kind word goes far. So everyday deeds of Ubuntu.

Dr. Dave:
So Nobantu, thank you so much for sharing your wisdom and your time today, for helping us to learn more about Ubuntu and how we could put that into practice, especially here, well, and all over the world. I mean, it's something that we need, especially with a lot of the challenges that we have going on in the world.

So I would just like to thank you for giving us your time today.

And so in closing, I'd like to say thank you for listening to the KnolShare with Dr. Dave podcast. Our conversation today was about Ubuntu, and practicing Ubuntu will allow you to find yourself through relationship with others, to experience belonging and healing.

Belonging is a basic human need; it's an important part of who we are and how we find identity. So I hope this learning experience prompted you to seek to discover more ways to find your level of awesomeness through relationship with others.

I'd like here to say that the *KnolShare with Dr. Dave* podcast is streamed on Spotify, iTunes, Audible, and Google Play.

And the music for this podcast is done by my niece, Kiana Brown Hendrickson.

This podcast episode is copywritten 2022 by Dr. Dave Cornelius and knolshare.org.

And also, just in finally saying one more time, my expression of gratitude to Nobantu for giving her time today for our discussion. So grateful, so grateful.

Nobantu:
Thank you, Dr. Dave. Thank you.

WHY IS BELONGING IMPORTANT? A CONVERSATION WITH DR. DAVE AND TRACY TREACY

Podcast: *KnolShare with Dr. Dave,* found on Spotify, iTunes, Audible, and Google Play

VLog: https://vimeo.com/655703242

Dr. Dave:
Hey, hello and welcome to the *KnolShare with Dr. Dave* podcast. Hey, this is Dr. Dave Cornelius, your host, and I'm excited to be here with my friend, Tracy. Tracy, we're going to be talking about belonging and why it's important. And so earlier, we talked about putting up an episode per month as we begin to work on our book, *Belonging and Healing*. So Tracy Treacy, welcome. What's going on with you?

Tracy:
Dave, hey. Thank you. Good morning and life is good.

Dr. Dave:
Look at you. I am in that calm mode, just chill today. I don't know what's up with that, but I wanted to start off with a quote by Angela Maya.

Tracy:
Oh come on.

Dr. Dave:
By Maya Angelou.

Tracy:
Okay.

Dr. Dave:
And she says, "I long, as does every human being, to be at home wherever I find myself." So that's her context of belonging. And so, why is belonging important? Why do we care so much about belonging as human beings? What's the deal with that?

Tracy:
Heck if I know. It's innate; it's something we feel complete, in order to belong somewhere, that makes us feel complete. That makes us feel like we have some kind of anchor, some kind of grounding. It just, to feel like you belong kind of gives you some wholeness, some sense of being, right?

Dr. Dave:
Yeah. So that's what it is, a sense of being.

Tracy:
Yeah.

Dr. Dave:
So what story do you have from yourself about belonging? I know you and I have been having conversations about belonging.

Tracy:
Yeah.

Dr. Dave:
What about for you, specifically?

Tracy:
So there's different areas of belonging and different places and spaces. And for me, I think the most important belonging or sense of belonging that I have is familial belonging. And there's work belonging, there's family belonging, there's societal, so

there's different cultures, ethnicity, all of those, but familial belonging is pretty high up on the list for me. My relationships with the people that I share DNA with or have chosen to love, that's the most important.

Dr. Dave:
We share that in common. And so I was reflecting this week on a belonging story. And I can remember that as a kid, and I think it was maybe around three or four years old, this is how important this memory is in my life, is that my parents had gotten divorced and my mother went to work on another island. And so I remember as a kid missing my mother so much that I would put on my uncle's shoes and socks and I would be running down the street toward the pier on this island, trying to go find my mom.

Tracy:
Oh.

Dr. Dave:
So it's that sense of belonging, it's a familial, it's really, really deep for me. You know how you and I connect as brothers and sisters.

Tracy:
Yeah.

Dr. Dave:
So that is really important for me. So that kind of anchored my sense of belonging, from a very young age and in a very deep way.

Tracy:
And also to add to that gives a sense of ... And for people who don't have a family system that they feel like they belong to, I would hope that they are able to choose people that they feel

as if they're family with them and can belong in that sense. Because we don't always get the graciousness of having a family system that we're born into that we get along with, or feel accepted by, or like. But when we do, or when we choose those family systems or those people that we call family, there's this sense of: I feel important to these other people. It's important for me to be in this system to make this system better, or this system helps me to be better. And to go along with those lines of a family experience or memory, family reunions, big thing, right?

Dr. Dave:
Yeah.

Tracy:
Big thing in many cultures and families. And I have the joy, I guess I could say, of having over 100 first cousins. Right. And to actually know them by name and to be able to recognize them, and also get to know new cousins often as well that aren't first cousins, still in my life now, is kind of dope. Right?

Dr. Dave:
Yeah. That's huge.

Tracy:
So that to me, it's really, really important. And that sense of—I happen to come from a family that has a lot of pride in who they are as people. And not everybody has that, which I really, really want to impress that to people, to find your people, right? Be able to identify who that would be for you and to attempt to find that, and how do we find that is a whole other thing, right? We'll have a question, yeah, I got to find my people. How do I do that? If you have those people, let those people know that they're important to you.

Dr. Dave:
Yes.

Tracy:
Right? And that reciprocal sense of belonging is just so rich and valuable.

Dr. Dave:
Yeah. And so, I'm going to describe, based on Harari, who wrote the book *Sapiens,* and he described belonging as an intimate community where people know each other well and depend on each other for survival. So he talks about *Homo sapiens* banning together to create a community for survival and protection. But I think it's also for us to connect, physically, spiritually, emotionally, and losing that sense of belonging sometimes creates this immense sense of anxiety. And I think that's some of the things that you're touching on in terms of letting people know they're important, because sometimes when we get separated, for whatever reasons, it could really create a lot of anxiety in our lives and make things really difficult for us to function within our society. So what are your thoughts around that?

Tracy:
Well, it just goes right along with what we've been saying. To be able to find the ... Really finding yourself so that you can find your people.

Dr. Dave:
Yeah.

Tracy:
And understanding that you are a result of a lot of things that's happened to you that you've experienced. And being okay with that, that that has nothing to do with your ability or your worth to belong to someone or a group. And that is

a survival instinct, which is what you're describing. To be alone for humans is to die, because you think about a baby and you leave a baby by themselves, right? We need to belong somewhere, even sometimes it's shitty where we belong, but that interaction also helps us to grow. Without the interaction, we don't grow.

Dr. Dave:
Certainly, that's a fact. So, I just noticed that we're kind of wearing the same, similar color.

Tracy:
Yeah. I saw that we were twinning. Yeah, yeah, yeah.

Dr. Dave:
What's up with that? Is that belonging or what?

Tracy:
I don't know, but that leads to that calm. I meditated and worked out this morning, so I'm in the ah.

Dr. Dave:
I like that.

Tracy:
And I didn't change clothes, so there is that.

Dr. Dave:
Okay. Okay. Yeah.

Tracy:
Right, right, right.

Dr. Dave:
And then there's that.

Tracy:
There is that.

Dr. Dave:
There you go. But when we think of, when we get outside of just the familial aspect of it and we're looking into the work space, where people could really come there and be their genuine self, well, and they should change after their workout. And so it's ... What is that? What are your thoughts around that in terms of people in the workplace needing to be authentic, needing to bring their whole selves, needing to feel like they belong in that space, to be able to produce value for the company that they work for? What's your thoughts?

Tracy:
Yeah. You touched on this in the blog, right? So it's about that workplace allowing that authenticity to show and to support that authenticity of that person. And sometimes we don't even know who we authentically are because we have been walking around masking who we are in order to fit in with groups that we think we want to belong [to] and we're supposed to belong to in order to fit that mold of what that group is. So uncovering that authentic self is a job in and of itself. Once that's touched on, for you to be able to be confident in who you are as authentically as you can and you walk into a workplace and that's not supported, that doesn't make for a very good relationship. Because you're bound to have to wear a mask in order to fit in. Not very healthy for mental health, right? You talked about anxiety earlier?

Dr. Dave:
Yeah, yeah.

Tracy:
That's that anxiety producing thing, right?

Dr. Dave:
Yeah.

Tracy:
So the workplaces have to work on creating an environment that people can show up authentically.

Dr. Dave:
Well, which is true and companies are trying, because it's not what I would think, it's not their core competency. So if you work for a tech company, they're about building software. If you work for a clothing company ... And the thing is, is how do we develop these, what I call innate human skills? These are skills that we lose touch with at some point, because I'm thinking about ... You brought up the concept of a baby not being able to survive alone, but those skills [of] belonging and how we interact with each other start at that level. Right?

Tracy:
Mm-hmm [affirmative].

Dr. Dave:
And it progresses throughout time. I was just looking at this belonging barometer from Ernst & Young, and so I was just going to read off some of the statistics that we have going on here. And so—

Tracy:
That's statistics.

Dr. Dave:
Statistics.

Tracy:
Yes, there you go.

Dr. Dave:
Yes, well you know I have to have surgery next week.

Tracy:
I understand. You can say stats, we know what that is.

Dr. Dave:
Early in the morning. So what they're saying is 56% of all the respondents that they spoke to—and they spoke to about a hundred people, adult Americans who are professionals—and they said they felt somewhat that they belong and they feel trusted and respected. And so even baby boomers, are you a baby boomer?

Tracy:
Nope.

Dr. Dave:
Okay. Nope. Is your husband a baby boomer?

Tracy:
Yep.

Dr. Dave:
Yep. So I'm a baby boomer at the very tail end, the very last [minute] of it. So we feel, about 63% of us feel that we feel somewhat that we belong and the gen Xers are only at 56%, then the millennials. So you can see it's decreasing over time in terms of how people feel they belong. What's going on with that in this modern time where as we get to the gen Xers and the millennials, we started to feel less and less connected to the workspace or the people that we work with? What do you think?

Tracy:
Yeah, I don't know if this is definitive, but I mean, this is just wondering out loud. I wonder if it's because of how people are beginning to work differently and how some of the workplaces are doing the construct of the old guard, I guess we could call it that, and moving and evolving with how important belonging is to productivity in the workplace. And there's a shift, and for the companies to catch up with that shift. And this is

corporations. Small companies may have it in the bag and [are] doing a little bit more. Family owned businesses, who knows. But if we look at corporations, there's an evolutionary shift, and some millennials are not buying into that corporate bullshit, and they're just like, "I'm going to be and do on my own so that I can create a space of belonging for others." So I don't know. I don't have a specific answer, but I'm just throwing out things that could be going on.

Dr. Dave:
Well yeah, the needs are different definitely.

Tracy:
Absolutely.

Dr. Dave:
As I look, think about my own career, we try to fit in. We try to do whatever was necessary to be a part of that culture, which meant for people like me code switching was a thing, and we have to learn how to fit into that space and speak the lingo and the behavior and everything else that was part of the culture there. What the millennials and younger they're ... They want do their own space; they want to be their authentic self and to be able to survive there.

Tracy:
Yeah. And I think when you mention code switch, that is something people of a certain generation knew that it was necessary to do in order to survive where they were.

Dr. Dave:
Yeah.

Tracy:
Because of the mainstream's view of things, that in-between generation, not millennials, but what is that, Zers? Gen Zers?

Dr. Dave:
And Xers and the Zers?

Tracy:
Xers, Zers, Yers, those people.

Dr. Dave:
Yeah, somewhere in there.

Tracy:
It started pushing back at that. As black women, we talk about the hair. If you can't wear braids at work and all of that stuff. Now it's like "excuse me, this is my hair and I do and wear with it what I please. It's on my body." Right?

Dr. Dave:
Yeah.

Tracy:
That's my choice, right? So there's more of a pushback and that's just an example, not a ... It's a long term example. So I think the pushback is helping the corporations reluctantly evolve so that code switching may not be a thing for people to do anymore. It may not be the best advice for baby boomers to give to millennials in order to make it in the corporate workplace.

Dr. Dave:
Well, I don't even think that we should give ourselves that advice; it's not healthy, right? Wearing a mask, and it's something that we want to get beyond. But if we wanted to talk about belonging in the space, in the workspace, in the work environment, whether that's a mom and pop, it's a corporation, how do we start talking about the purpose, the why of belonging in the organization? What kind of actions do we take to share the why? Because oftentimes, we may run into

these programs and said, "Oh, we're going to have a belonging, a DEI program and stuff," but what is the purpose? Why is this important?

Tracy:
I think the individual companies have to deem it important because it is important because our world is, I like to call it a salad buffet instead of a melting pot, because there's all these distinct differences on this salad and you want to taste the crunch, you want to taste the salty, you want to taste the whatever, right? In order for that to go well together, you have to appreciate each thing individually. That has to be something that a company wants to do. I don't know how we can make a company do that other than to look at society at large and the dissonance that we see in areas and topics and how folks are just not getting along.

Dr. Dave:
Or connecting, right? I mean, to me, that's the importance of belonging as well is how well do we connect and have a common and shared purpose in the space that we are, whether it's at work or a place of worship. So I was thinking as we're putting the blog or the article together around some simple tools, like what I call employee net promoter scores [that] are really beginning to sense the sentiment of people in the organization. That's one context, right? Let's gather that information just to see how can we be informed by the people who are actually in that space? And even though that would help us just start telling the story, and then we could start to create what I like to think of these [as] different wonderful events that we could have of where we start to create that space of belonging, right? So I was thinking of things like can we have an open mic? Maybe spoken word, wouldn't that be fun? Yeah? And people come up and share why do you think belonging is important to them for—

Tracy:

Yeah. Interesting way to do it. Storytelling is a thing. So part of what I did in one of my births of life, I guess, I worked with domestic violence perpetrators, and they were all males. All male domestic violence perpetrators, and we did a lot of healing with this group of people because what we found is that there was a lot of trauma in their background. So we worked to work with their trauma to help heal their trauma and we would do ritual work with them and we would actually go through some healing rituals that

... that help them get from "I believe that what I'm doing is right, because I'm protecting myself and this is how I express how I feel" to ... "Maybe that is not so right and my violence was causing pain to others and myself." At the end of this program, we would have an open mic. So when you said that, that made me think of ... These men, these brothers would get up and write poems, story tell, talk about their journey, the whole bit. And we would invite people from the community to come in.

And most of these, if not all these, men were on probation or parole, so they were within the system. So we would invite judges, probation officers, people that ... treatment facilities ... that they had to show up for a while [when] they were doing the program. It really shifts the way the criminal justice system, the people on the other side, viewed their clients because they were our clients as well as theirs. And they saw them as more human.

So I think there may be something to that. Storytelling, just being in a room to share. Restorative justice is another thing, those kinds of things really help to promote listening and leveling the playing field in that we all go through stuff.

Dr. Dave:
Go ahead.

Tracy:
No, go ahead. Yeah.

Dr. Dave:
No, it's just bringing us back to the core of being human beings, right? That we all have stuff. And the other thing I was thinking about beyond ... Open mic is storytelling, but we could tell stories through posters, kind of vision posters that we could put different imagery of what belonging means to us as something more permanent. Not even permanent, but it could be more of a display. Think of, we're going to a museum of some sort, that the workspace also becomes, or that space becomes a museum for the art that's being published.

Tracy:
Which is another thing we did. We did that exact thing, right?

Dr. Dave:
Yeah.

Tracy:
And so those forms of display really help the person understand how they belong. And it helps them to be in the [inaudible] because that might change as a person heals. Some of those images and ideas may change and that will help them see their progression, see their movement toward being more whole. And some people feel like I need to feel whole in order to belong somewhere. And that's not always necessarily true.

Dr. Dave:
No.

Tracy:
Right? So I don't think we have to have all our shit together in order to belong somewhere.

Dr. Dave:
No. Well, I want you to tell me when you have all your shit together. So I'm never there, so.

Tracy:
Exactly. And that's what I was going to say, because many of us who don't have our shit together belong to each other, right? So it's okay, right?

Dr. Dave:
So the third thing I thought about was this thing we call Open Space, where people bring topics that they want to cover. And then they gather in a room, small pods of individuals having these discussions, and they're capturing what's being shared in that space.

Tracy:
Right.

Dr. Dave:
So that's another way of thinking like, how do we begin to share the purpose of belonging where it's not just driven by HR?

Tracy:
Mm-hmm [affirmative].

Dr. Dave:
The human resource group, but it's really engaging the whole community to be a part of the conversation, such that when we talk about ... Here's why belonging is important. We have many voices and I think Open Space Technology ... You've been through an Open Space.

Tracy:
Yeah.

Dr. Dave:
At one of our agile events, and so you could see how that works, right? And using the wisdom of the crowd to participate. And so we could call it the festival of belonging, what do you think?

Tracy:
No.

Dr. Dave:
Come on. What would you call it?

Tracy:
I don't know, but it wouldn't be that.

Dr. Dave:
I would love to hear what you come up with.

Tracy:
Yeah. I'll have to sleep on that one, but festival of belonging, I don't know, bro.

Dr. Dave:
Yeah. I can see it. Yeah.

Tracy:
Okay. What would it look like? Tell me what it would look like.

Dr. Dave:
I just gave you three: posters, open mic, Open Space.

Tracy:
So it would be that museum idea.

Dr. Dave:
Well, it's the museum, it's the open mic storytelling. It's open space as an event, so that's the festival. Everyone comes and I

was even thinking more along the lines of, "Hey, come in your authentic garb, bring some food." Really make it a festival.

Tracy:
So this sounds like ... I don't know if you remember this thing we had, Holiday Folk Fair?

Dr. Dave:
Yeah.

Tracy:
Do you remember that? That's what that sounds like to me, it sounds like a Renaissance fair. It sounds like a State Fair. It sounds like a—

Dr. Dave:
It's a human fair.

Tracy:
... Okay, Dave. It's a human fair.

Dr. Dave:
It's going to be some creative ideas that are floating around that we could make something interesting and fun.

Tracy:
Yeah. Creative is one thing, but corny, come on.

Dr. Dave:
Oh boy, I'm corny. That's good. We belong.

Tracy:
There you go. Exactly.

Dr. Dave:
I was just thinking of this as an opportunity for people to experience and learn and share about what belonging means together. It's just one model; there are many different ways we could approach this. What?

Tracy:
Yeah. And I think there are areas where we do have that, where people sell their different wares and about their different cultures and some kind of markets and stuff. So something on a belonging scale, in that sense. Okay.

Dr. Dave:
Because I think sometimes ... And as I'm spending more time reading about different people's context of belonging.

Tracy:
Yeah.

Dr. Dave:
And this is important to you, you believe in somatic healing. So one of the things that's coming up is that it's not just about the psychological aspect, it's also in our bones, it's in our flesh, it's in our blood and being able to see and touch and write. And whether we're using some type of physical metaphors to help us understand and what belonging is, it helps us with healing.

Tracy:
Mm-hmm [affirmative].It's about that release from the battle, right? So if I'm code switching at a job and it causes all of this anxiety in me to do that, and I go home, I've got to release that. If I don't, it just gets stored up. And who knows what that can turn into, right? That's what disease is all about. Right? There's a disease in the body. So who knows what all of that kind of anxiety can turn into? And certain peoples and cultures do know what that anxiety turns into, right? The high blood pressure to diabetes, all of those kinds of things. We have to release that on a certain level and it's a cellular release, Dave. It is, as you said, bones, blood, the whole bit.

Dr. Dave:
DNA.

Tracy:
And when you ... Ancestral, definitely it comes down through the ancestors and through the generations, right? What we can do, like a really quick thing we can do is when we do the thing that we know is not authentic to us, begin to recognize where you feel that in your body. You may not know it right now because you're so used to doing it, but if you slow down enough and you do the thing, you're going to feel it somewhere in your body. Take note of that and then begin to focus on that part of the body and ask that part of the body. You [are] going to be talking to your body, "Okay body, okay belly, what do I need to do to release this out of there? What kind of messaging am I getting?" And begin to start having that dialogue with the body. Go ahead.

Dr. Dave:
Go ahead.

Tracy:
Yeah. So the book I'm looking at, Bessel van der Kolk, *The Body Keeps the Score,* right? That is a book that is becoming much more popular in mainstream society, but it talks about how stuff is stored in the body. And the body responds to the stuff in some kind of way that might be maladaptive, as we move through the world. So listening to our body is really important. What we've learned though, if we ... That sense of belonging and the baby, what we've learned though, sometimes some people feel like their bodies are not safe.

Dr. Dave:
Yes.

Tracy:
That's a whole nother level of things, because you can't get in your body if you don't think it's safe, right?

Dr. Dave:
Well, you can't appreciate your body either, if you don't think it's safe.

Tracy:
Well, yeah.

Dr. Dave:
Well, I'm just saying. But I was just thinking of one of the exercises that this author, I can't remember his name, but he was talking about, he says, What's humming and rubbing your belly?

Tracy:
Mm-hmm [affirmative].

Dr. Dave:
And I know you used the term corny, but I was thinking, Hey, that is pretty interesting, to sit down and as you're dealing with some level of stress, of rubbing your belly and humming and how that helps to release the stress and the anxiety.

Tracy:
That's not corny at all. Well, a thing for people that if they're feeling really anxious and out of sorts, to make sure that they know that they're in their body, and sometimes all you need to do is tap your index finger to your thumb, or apply pressure. It's like an acupressure point, just so that you know, I'm here. It helps ground you. And there's a concept called tapping where, right along this area, if you tap, reach you in your body. It's about settling your nervous system so that you can be in your body. That's super important when you talk about somatic healing and that somatic connection.

Dr. Dave:
Well, we had to go through it. Just in our conversation today, and talk[ing] about belonging in multiple facets, and how we

could also help to adjust ourselves into a space of belonging. So, as we talk about reflecting and the purpose of, why belonging is important, what do you want people to walk away with, in terms of things that is memorable or that resonates with them, or just ideas that they may take away, some nuggets from this topic today?

Tracy:
And we've covered quite a bit in this little bit of half hour, right? Recognizing if you feel like you don't belong, it's okay. Acknowledge that, and don't say, "I don't belong because I suck." That's not the answer and that's not the reason. It might have to start with yourself, and that is the last conversation we had, that somatic part. Feel as if you belong to yourself, and you don't have to be a 100% actualized or any of that, just begin to say, "I can own my shit. I am me, and I'm okay to be here." Just start with something like that. That may not sound good for some people, because people may be thinking, "Yeah right, I'm about two steps away from just getting the heck out of here," but be okay with belonging to yourself, with whatever that looks like. And then, think about where you want to belong, like community-wise, and then move to that, and then if you're working and you don't feel like you belong at work, are there real steps that can be taken for that to happen?

What I've noticed though, Dave, is if work is a place where you don't feel safe, if you build up all those other areas in your life to feel as if you belong, work does not become as much of a problem to feel like you don't belong, because you've got that richness in other areas.

Dr. Dave:
I agree with that in the context that yes, because we're bringing another dimension, a full dimension of ourselves to work. The other thing that we have to be mindful of is that we spend one

third of our lives, each day, sometimes up to six, seven days a week, in that toxic place.

Tracy:
And we're spending more time in that place than we do at home with our loved ones.

Dr. Dave:
Our community.

Tracy:
That's a tough one, because you say, let's not make it an HR problem, but it might have to be an HR issue right now for it to begin to happen, and then we can work within the departments and all of that other stuff. You know, I don't know.

Dr. Dave:
So, I'm not saying it's not an HR problem, I said, it's not only an HR problem. It's a whole organization problem that we need everyone to participate and bring their ideas to the table, even if HR is the agency that's helping to move this through to enterprise. We need people, we need people's ideas, and we need to make it a community thing, and that's why we love going to these different little festival things. Don't even try it. I mean, I remember you going to some festival stuff.

Tracy:
Not a festival of humans.

Dr. Dave:
Of course that was a festival of humans. I remember Summerfest, that's a festival, all sorts of different things happening there, but that's where I'm coming from, from festival in context.

Tracy:
I get it. I get it. I'm just giving you shit.

Dr. Dave:
I know. I'm bringing it back.

Tracy:
And you mentioned Summerfest, that's a music festival, and then there's other ones. There's Bonnaroo, there's Lilith Fair. I don't know all the others.

Dr. Dave:
There's so many things.

Tracy:
South by Southwest. There's so many music festivals that bring people together, and that's great. And I think what we're talking about, is how do we get that to go on a deeper level, like leveling up with that, on a deeper level, in places with where we work.

Dr. Dave:
Or even in our own community. It doesn't even just have to be work. It could be, "Hey, we live in this neighborhood with a number of thousands of people or hundreds of people. Can we do something like this? Is it possible?"

Tracy:
Well, and the reason I said work is because of that eight to 10 hours a day that we're spending with people that might be causing us that anxiety that we're not releasing, and if we can have a space at homeBessel van der Kolk

Great! That's it, exactly. ... space at home to do those things, or to release and to safe, all the things, really, and it may look goofy, but if you're sitting at your desk and you're doing this, nobody's going to know what you're doing.

Dr. Dave:
Nope.

Tracy:
And what you're doing is you're calming yourself down. Right. Even rubbing, like you're doing. You can rub any parts of your body, and you see my chakra banner behind me?

Dr. Dave:
I see your chakra banners.

Tracy:
So I do chakra work, and even focusing on those chakra areas can really help ground you in your body. It's about really feeling safe in your own skin, so that you can feel safe being in your skin, wherever you are.

Dr. Dave:
That's very important, and I think that's a good place to land, being safe in your own skin, wherever you are.

So, let me lead out and say, belonging is so important to our existence as human beings. It's one of those things that we seek frequently.

And so I would like to say thank you for listening to the *KnolShare with Dr. Dave* podcast. I like to say thank you to Tracy Treacy for partnering in our conversation, and we continue to do this wonderful collaboration.

And so you could find the *KnolShare with Dr. Dave* podcast on Spotify, Audible, iTunes, and Google Play. Want to do a shout out to Kiana Brown Hendrickson for the theme music and say that this podcast is copyright 2021, Dr. Dave Cornelius and Knolshare.org, and you know, Tracy, one more thing before we leave?

Tracy:
Yo homie, what? What is that?

Dr. Dave:
I don't know. I'm asking you, do you have one more thing?

Tracy:
One more thing? Just be good with who you are. We are, you are individually perfect just the way you are. You may have had to learn and adapt to things because of what you've been dealt.

Dr. Dave:
Certainly.

Tracy:
That's it.

THE LANGUAGE OF BELONGING: A CONVERSATION WITH DR. DAVE AND TRACY TREACY

Podcast: *KnolShare with Dr. Dave,* found on Spotify, iTunes, Audible, and Google Play

VLog: https://vimeo.com/666327987

Dr. Dave:
All right. Hello and welcome to the *KnolShare with Dr. Dave* podcast. This is Dr. Dave Cornelius, your host. We're continuing a conversation of belonging and healing with my guest, Tracy Treacy from D & S Healing Center.

Tracy:
Woo.

Dr. Dave:
Yay, the thing is when we talk about sticks and stones can break my bones, but words could never harm me, to me that's just partially true because words matter. I think words can be harmful, especially for people in need of belonging, and even if they don't have a need for belonging, I think words can be harmful. And so for me, the word that always shows up is the N-word, which I think is a harmful word, and I said, no matter if it ends with A, personally, I don't want to continue to prolong long the use of a word that has been used to dehumanize my family and community, and other people may have a different

opinion, but that's where I stand and I'm sticking to it. What about you, Tracy? What word rubs you the wrong way?

Tracy:
That's what you feel, and you're sticking with it.

Dr. Dave:
That's right; it's all about that.

Tracy:
I don't know if a word rubs me the wrong way. I think it's the intention behind the word that gets me or who it's coming from because if somebody off the street calls me something or says something to me that I'm like, "You know what, maybe they're having a bad day." I got a little bit more empathy and compassion for them, but if somebody who loves me and is part of my space where I feel like I belong, and they say something, that probably hits deeper than any ... The N-word ... I don't know, maybe I'm just numb to it. I've heard it so many times; it's like what the "F&&k" ever.

Dr. Dave:
Right.

Tracy:
That's not my issue that you're calling me that, or that you think that, that's your issue, but when someone says or has some meaning beside something that loves me or that say they love me, then that hurts, that affects me.

Dr. Dave:
I could totally relate to that. So, I was reading something from MIT recently and a study that they did, they were talking about we crave relationships in the same region of the brain that we crave food, that's belonging, and we experience social exclusion in the same brain area that we experience physical pain. So, what I'm thinking about is language is very powerful,

and we could use it to divide us, unite us, and sharing the same language builds camaraderie between individuals and it helps us support the shared knowledge base and words used. So, what language can be used to encourage more belonging in your opinion?

Tracy:
That's a lot.

Dr. Dave:
I know it is.

Tracy:
What came to my brain immediately is the language of love, and I guess what I mean by that is when you ... And, we don't always do this because we're not always in a place to be conscious or mindful enough to do it, but speaking from the heart, as opposed to waiting to hear what someone's saying, being present, all of those things that we talk about in mindfulness, being present in the moment, taking a breath before you respond and then respond from a place of love: that's what came to mind for me. To me, it's that simple. And in order to respond from a place of love, we may have to feel that we've been loved and we are loved, so that we can give and receive it, and I guess that goes back to that belonging.

Dr. Dave:
Love is one of my favorite words because my translation of it is very biblical in the sense that I'm talking about being patient and kind, and if I could bring those two aspects of my humanity into the conversation, into the environment, the space, then that's the work that we need to do to help, to encourage belonging. So for this year, my word for 2022 is kindness, and so that's going to be the mantra that I'll be chanting all the way through December 31st of 2022.

Tracy:
All right, so I can always remind you when you're being a butthead, I can go, "Kindness."

Dr. Dave:
Yeah.

Tracy:
All right.

Dr. Dave:
You could always bring it up and I will work my way back into the great plan of being kind.

Tracy:
Yes.

Dr. Dave:
I'll poke you with the same thing. Do you have a word that you want to claim for 2022?

Tracy:
I haven't thought of it in the context of having a word to cling to for the year. I don't know—

Dr. Dave:
Not embrace?

Tracy:
I guess it's the other word, maybe patience because I think I may have been wired with an over-abundance of patience, and that's something I always continue to have, grace and patience with others, so maybe patience for self.

Dr. Dave:
Well, you need both, just like you need love for self to be able to love others. You need patience with oneself to be patient with others. It's so interesting that we have to give something

to ourselves, so we know what the experience is like to give it to others if we can.

Tracy:
How else are we, right? And, then that's the hardest thing for a lot of people is to treat themselves with kindness and patience and grace, and our behaviors aren't always clean and we respond unconsciously to a lot of things, but we don't know how that's affecting other people and part of all of that is that being able to hear from other people how my actions affect you with patience, with kindness, with all of those things as well because shit, we're human.

Dr. Dave:
Yep.

Tracy:
It's always a journey and a thing.

Dr. Dave:
We probably will come up with an AI that's capable of doing all of that stuff consistently.

Tracy:
Oh God.

Dr. Dave:
I know I would get that response back from you.

Tracy:
Oh my God.

Dr. Dave:
I knew I would.

Tracy:
Patience, I'm having patience with you, yes, patience.

Dr. Dave:

The language of belonging to me is a tone of invitation, this voice of acceptance and maybe a sound of empathy, and I was just thinking about some of the language that I may have used with my kids and at times where I had to go back and apologize. "Oh my God, I'm sorry that I've traumatized you and maybe not make you feel like you belong." And so, I'm going like ... Thinking about the language, that abuse of my kids at times and how also ... Because there's two sides of it. There's one side of it: we're helping them to create this stable sense of identity, so that they become capable adults, and then there's the other side of it is where I've used those language that I've had to go back and apologize. So, I'm thinking about how could we, or how would we introduce language and help people to find their way forward? Because to me, it's building a stable sense of identity, enabling them to become capable adults is part of helping them to find a way forward. So, what do you think?

Tracy:

I want to just applaud what you said, and I think that's something that needs to be highlighted and needs to be validated is that when we harm our children in some kind of way, when we say something that is hurtful, that we go back and apologize, and as parents, we don't feel like we need to apologize sometimes because we're the parent, and it's really difficult to hear that from somebody we love and we've made so many ... The word sacrifice has such a negative connotation, but love sacrifices. We've made so many allowances in our lives to provide space for these beings that we're responsible for that when we harm that being, it's so difficult to hear it from them because they may not always have a language to share with us that they've been harmed, and it may come off and out a way that we are not ready to hear it.

And, then we as parents go, "We're the authority. You're not supposed to talk to me like that," or something, that kind of garbage, instead of just being like, "Wow, this little person's human, maybe little, but they're human." And to have that space of respect to be like, "Shoot, that was really jacked up what I said or my response was not what I really meant," those kind of things and really apologizing. So, I applaud that because that's not a regular thing for us to hear that parents apologize to their children.

Dr. Dave:

Well, and I would say sometimes in the type of family that we may have grown up in and how our parents were affected by their upbringing ... I grew up in the West Indies, and I keep telling people that you grew up in the West Indies, the language there could be harsh sometimes from parents, and over time, I've learned that it's a form of protection, and because they're like, "Oh my God, we have come through this trauma of slavery and all of the other negative things that comes from that," that it's a sense of protectionism with some of the harsh language that in a way they're thinking about how it helps move you forward. Right? Preparing you for the rough world.

Tracy:

Right. So that gets back to the other part of that and do we support people to help them move forward? And because of certain backgrounds of people and experiences and ancestral legacies, and I get because you said slavery, I can go in that space, right. Because of the slave experience, there's also learned behaviors that we've gotten from being enslaved that we transfer into our systems and our life with harsh language and corporal punishment and things like that. So from that survival space, we feel we're really helping strengthen our offspring to get out into the world to be able to handle stuff, which is about that, right, that protectiveness, when with all that loving stuff that comes with that, that needs to be equally as stressed as the other stuff. And I think that's where some of that, how I can help move, like if we're talking about our kids, right, how do I keep that discipline thing going, yet let them know that I love them no matter what and I got their back?

And this might sound a little hokey and this is something that's just in pop culture that I'm going to throw in is about the love languages. Right? If you know your child's love language, then maybe that is a way to help them to begin to have ownership, to feel like they belong to themselves and they can belong in community. And that can maybe help support them to move forward.

Dr. Dave:
Yeah, because one thing I will say to my son, right, is that "look, I love you from the day that I saw you being born and I love you to this day," and I just give him a big hug. I said, "No matter what you do, no matter what, no matter what you say, just know that I love you from the deepest core of who I am." And to me, just that in terms of wherever he's stuck, it helps to move him forward.

Tracy:
And I'm just going to add to that because we live in such a world that's so visual and no matter how you look, I'm going to love you. Right. Because physically we could ... And I guess I'm saying that more as a woman, because of how much pressure is put on how women are supposed to look and all the things that society puts onto us as attractive, right? And no matter how my child looks, I'm going to love them and let them know that. Right? In addition to, as a parent, right, there's that fine line of "I really love you, but I want you to be healthy too." We do that thing in our brains, right?

Dr. Dave:
Yeah, I get that. I'm glad you put your earrings on, so no matter how you look.

Tracy:
Exactly, right?

Dr. Dave:
Exactly, right?

Tracy:
Exactly. That presentation. Yep.

Dr. Dave:
Yeah.

Tracy:
And here I am plucking at my hair—

Dr. Dave:
I hear you.

Tracy:
All the things, yeah.

Dr. Dave:
You got to do it.

Tracy:
Yeah.

Dr. Dave:
So workplace, I think that shared language enables us to build a sustainable community that's welcoming. So I was thinking of quoting Adam Grant and he said, "A workplace is a community—a place where people bond around shared values, feel valued as human beings, and have a voice in decisions that affect them." So to me, where we're talking about culture, so

I'm saying what are some ways that language helps to shape culture that enables belonging?

Tracy:
Yeah, so I was just going to backpedal what I said, "No matter what you look like, I just want you to be healthy too." That had nothing to do with any type of anything except for psychological health, right. Because you can look at a person and be like, "Ooh, I don't know if you may look a little depressed or something." That's what I mean by look, nothing physical look, right? Or health. So the language to help shape, I mean, you know that hokey bullshit, positive affirmations and saying things that'll gas somebody up, sincerely though. Right? Because are you blowing smoke up my ass, are you gassing me up just to get something or is it really sincere? Right. And since we're talking parent child, it's important to let your children know that what they're good at they're damn, damn good at, and if it's in their pocket, it's in their pocket. Right. And not to doubt that. And even the things that they aren't good at, still fricking try them. That's okay. And it's okay to not be good at something. Right? Yeah.

Dr. Dave:
Yep. It's all about what you learn. So as we're trying to shape this culture, right, with language, I think it's such an important aspect of where we live, where we work, the whole community aspect of it. So I'm trying to figure out what ways, what language could we use to help build up our culture in such a way that we have that tone of acceptance and the tone of invitation and voice of acceptance and there's empathy, that we walk in there and you go like, you have that song from *Friends*: we want to go where everyone knows your name. I'm being hokey, right?

Tracy:
Oh, you mean—

Dr. Dave:
That's culture.

Tracy:
No, that's not *Friends*. That's *Cheers*.

Dr. Dave:
That's *Cheers*.

Tracy:
Yes.

Dr. Dave:
Right. *Cheers*. It's *Cheers*. That's right.

Tracy:
It's *Cheers*. Right.

Dr. Dave:
It's *Cheers*. Right. Do you think of that song in your mind every time I want to go where everyone knows my name? Right. And so that is a language that's helping to shape a certain culture, right, in *Cheers*. So how's that coming across in your world or in your mind of what language we could use to build that up more, beside Norm sitting at the end of the bar, "Give me a beer."

Tracy:
Hey Dave, that's what we're doing. You walk in and everybody says, "Dave."

Dr. Dave:
Yeah. Or "Tray."

Tracy:
We all know this inclusivity, right?

Dr. Dave:
Yeah.

Tracy:
Duh.

Dr. Dave:
Yeah, but I think not just the feeling of, but the language of, right? So you come in you go like, "I'm Tray, what's going on?" Big hugs. It's like, "Lovely earrings."

Tracy:
Okay. Enough with the earrings.

Dr. Dave:
Come on.

Tracy:
And they don't match. I don't know if you noticed.

Dr. Dave:
I didn't even know that.

Tracy:
This one's smaller than this one because I lost each pair of the opposite.

Dr. Dave:
Now I can see, now I can see.

Tracy:
So I'm just wearing them together.

Dr. Dave:
Yeah. But I think there's some cool stuff going on. I was just thinking about to Steve the other day and allowing your son's bandmates or friends to come hang out at your crib. Right. And to me, what was that language all about? I could just imagine what Steve was saying to them to shape this culture. Like, "Hey man, it's cool. You belong here." Right. I wonder what he was saying to them. Did he tell you?

Tracy:
Yeah, I don't even know if it was the language. It was the feeling. It was the vibe, it was the—

Dr. Dave:
The vibe.

Tracy:
Yeah, they got here and no one was home, so we let them know how to get in the house. And young dude went and took a shower and set off the smoke alarm and it was hilarious. Right? So he texts us and he was like, "I set off the smoke alarm, blah, blah, blah." And we both just responded laughing because it's something our son has done often in the past.

Dr. Dave:
Right. Yeah.

Tracy:
Right?

Dr. Dave:
Yeah.

Tracy:
I think it was just being able to be for him to text us and be like, "Oh, crap, this is what I did" or communicate with us instead of through our son in order to navigate how to do what they do.

So it was a vibe. It was our son, or both of our children, know them even extending that to their friends was already in the language that you belong. It's accepted. It's all inclusive. And they were from all walks, shapes, textures of the world. Right? And there were six of them.

Dr. Dave:
Six.

Tracy:
Yeah. There were six. So bedrooms, basement, everything was sleeping quarters. And I cooked all the meals and it was just really ... I don't know if we said a whole lot to say yeah, it was a feeling. It was, "You come in my house and you make yourself at home."

Dr. Dave:
That's beautiful because that just walks us right into the next topic about the power of nonverbal communication. Right. That there's a signal of love. You're talking about patience and kindness in an abundant way

... that is widely available to all, so all of the understanding, right—

Tracy:
Yeah.

Dr. Dave:
... that is said in silence needs no words.

Tracy:
Right.

Dr. Dave:
So when I'm thinking about nonverbal communication, let's talk about, how does that signal that you belong here. I mean, we kind of just touched upon it with those six beautiful creative people.

Tracy:
Yeah.

Dr. Dave:
You know?

Tracy:
Yeah.

Dr. Dave:
Just the laughter, right. The laughter alone itself.

Tracy:
Oh my gosh. The conversation around the kitchen table. And this isn't the first time we've hosted some colleagues of his. So it's just kind of a ... if our children refer them to us or they stay with us, then they know and we know that it's all good.

Dr. Dave:
Yeah.

Tracy:
Right?

Dr. Dave:
Yeah. For sure.

Tracy:
So the nonverbal, it's that openness, right?

Dr. Dave:
Yeah. And I'm sure it's also tone and pitch too, right? Because you guys didn't shriek at them.

Tracy:
Right.

Dr. Dave:
This probably was nice and calm. "Oh, that's okay. Let me tell you how you could solve this." Right?

Tracy:
Right. Well, no, I don't know if I ... well, maybe I did some of that, so they—

Dr. Dave:
No, I can hear you, "What? You did what?"

Tracy:
No, no. Well, I think in the ... I mean, this is something I've had, this muscle I've had to grow because in the past, my house, I was very protective of my house and pretty anal about how you move in my house and what happens within that space. There are still some guidelines that I have, right.

Dr. Dave:
Yeah. I know.

Tracy:
But not ... Shut up, but I'm not as ... I'm much more open now, not as rigid as I was, but I had to grow that muscle. And I think that's important to say, because if it doesn't come natural to us and it's a problem for other people, we have to examine what's making us do those things. So is it, we decide if it's something we want to adjust or if we are going to really stay steadfast with it? And that is a nonverbal thing as well, right?

Because if somebody comes into your space and you are nonverbal, and I do this with clients a lot, if it's ... I mean, we know the arm folding thing, right? When we just fold our arms, and if I'm standing here with you and I'm doing this and we're talking, I am so disinterested, right? That's a nonverbal.

But if I'm here and I'm engaged and I'm there and I'm open to what you're saying ... And as older people, I guess, because all of this is multi-generational, we may need to be more mindful of listening instead of coming off as, "I know, because I'm older," and that all that nonverbal stuff comes across and facial expressions and body language. And I mean, yeah.

Dr. Dave:
You rolled your eyes, Tracy.

Tracy:
Right. You know? I have done that a lot with you.

Dr. Dave:
Yes, yes.

Tracy:
I will admit in our interactions.

Dr. Dave:
Well, because we know each other so well that we get to be like who we are with each other, right?

Tracy:
Right, right.

Dr. Dave:
Yes.

Tracy:
And then how do you respond to that? When I roll my eyes, you roll yours back. Or you're like, "Whatever," right?

Dr. Dave:
Yeah.

Tracy:
And there's that belonging because we feel as if we belong

Dr. Dave:
Yep, yep.

Tracy:
We can do those things. Then when there's conflict, we can talk about that, right?

Dr. Dave:
Yeah. I mean, that's the beauty of belonging, of being able to create that space. So looking at the flip side of that, now it's

like, how about nonverbal communications that will make people feel like they don't belong? That's another aspect and I notice sometimes, that it's where I am not giving them my full self so I'm partially in, and I'm not fully in, and then my head has turned somewhere else. So, it's some of those nonverbal communication signals that I like to hear more about us just to explore. What are some of those things that really get people feel like, "Oh, geez, I better go somewhere else"?

Tracy:
What does that make the person feel like? How does it make you feel when you walk into a space? How do you read if you belong in that space, when you walk in? How do you read if you don't belong in that space when you walk in?

Dr. Dave:
Well, I could tell you just from working in the tech space for a very long time, right? I mean, man, I used to live in Wisconsin. Wisconsin. And being an African American man from the Caribbean, walking into a space where I'm like the only black person in the software company, you get the looks, you get the cold shoulders, you get all of that, you know? And so you pick up on the vibe that like, "You really shouldn't be here. You don't belong here, man." Yeah. So I know what that's like. Just having those experiences, not only in Wisconsin, but also in Chicago and California and all over the United States that have had those experiences, because it's just like, "Hey man, what are you doing here? We don't have many of you doing the kind of work that we're doing, and this is really for us, so you don't really belong here," right?

Tracy:
Yeah. So what about the subtle, the more ... Not that that's not subtle, but what about the times where you may feel as if you

belong and then something happens that makes you go, "Huh? I guess I really don't."

Dr. Dave:
Hmm. Well, those subtle stuff are like crazy, right?

Tracy:
Yeah.

Dr. Dave:
And how it shows up. So it's interesting. Sometimes you're like ... Someone invites you into a social setting outside of work and you're in their space. Then you hear the whispers. You kind of like inadvertently [are] on the opposite side of a wall and you hear the whispers that are coming at you about like, "What? I can't believe they feel this way about me. I thought we were cool." And you realize that we aren't cool really, you know?

Tracy:
Yeah, yeah.

Dr. Dave:
So, that shows up, or even in terms of withholding information in your workspace. Hoarding information for power. I mean, that's just another form of nonverbal communication that makes you feel that you don't belong. So yeah. I mean, it's many experiences with this.

Tracy:
Yeah. And how do you navigate that? How do you work with ... because you have to build up some kind of armor to that so that it doesn't cripple you so that you can keep moving forward. Like what we're talking about. You need to keep moving forward. How do you navigate that?

Dr. Dave:

I think my sense of belonging growing up in a space where I was always encouraged to like, "Hey man, be the very best that you can be and no matter what. The sticks and stones could break my bones, but words could never harm you," is kind of the language that I learned growing up. So, "Hey man, go out there and be the very best."

And it helps you to build up what I call the id, your ego. I mean, and that id has been a great source of protection against some of that negativity that you may run into. So that's just the work that has happened over the years; I believe that if I'd grown up in a different space where I had to endure some of this negative harshness all my life, it would be different, but I grew up in a space where that wasn't the case.

I mean, sometimes I talk about knowing my, what I would call, like knowing speedy George, who was a police officer, but who would come and talk to us about different things when we were kids. Knowing the governors and people of color that makes you feel that, "Hey, you know what? I could get to that level and I could be damn effective no matter what and in spite of all of the negativity." So that has been helpful to prepare me to deal with the nonverbal communication, even the verbal communication that people want you to feel like you belong.

Tracy:

That's really good because it sounds like from your experience, you've had people who look like you in power positions—

Dr. Dave:

Yeah, yeah.

Tracy:

... and in important government, city—

Dr. Dave:
Yeah.

Tracy:
... even companywide positions because of the area you grew up in.

Dr. Dave:
And I think even more important, your teachers.

Tracy:
And teachers, yeah.

Dr. Dave:
Yeah. I mean, I think ... Well, you think about it. A third of your day as a kid is spent with your teachers, right?

Tracy:
Right. Right.

Dr. Dave:
... and your peers, and I think that was essential. Even the first experience was in Catholic schools with those nuns, but you still also had a great mixture of what they call lay teachers, who were teaching in all Catholic schools that gave us a different sense of who we are.

Tracy:
That is really interesting because I feel that parallel because I went to Catholic grade schools, and we had teachers that looked like me. And it was like, when I hear about ... Because I was a college professor for many years, and one of the inquiries that I would ask my students, or one of the questions is, when was the first time you had a teacher of color? And for both black and white students and not just black and white, but for many ethnic groups, I was their first teacher of color and this is college. We're talking you're an undergrad in college

in freshman, sophomore year, first time you've come across a teacher of color.

Dr. Dave:
And I could see that especially where you live. Where you live makes a big difference, that centering space.

Tracy:
So, that is really beautiful to hear that you had that experience, so that you could build and be able to flex that muscle when you came into spaces where you weren't quite accepted, or somebody was talking about you on the other side of whispers that you heard, and I don't know if we're getting into that, but I'd be really curious to know what those whispers said, what was being said.

Dr. Dave:
No, but it's interesting. Some of the whispers it's like, "I don't know who the hell he thinks he is. He's a blah, blah, blah, the N-word with E-R, instead of A, and blah, blah, blah, blah, blah," about this person. I'm going like, "What is that all about?"

Tracy:
Wow.

Dr. Dave:
But you build up your armor to be able to sustain some of that, and it still could be harmful to you, right?

Tracy:
Oh absolutely.

Dr. Dave:
If you keep getting all of that dumped on you, it starts to chip away at your armor. If you don't have a space to replenish that, that place of belonging, it's really hard.

Tracy:

Which goes back to that home life where we started and family of origin and the family you've made in your world at that point to belong there and to get that love because what we think psychologically is if the job is shit, that can be handled if everything else is going supportively for you. I don't want to get into how much is good and what's well and what's not well, but supportive. If you've got supportive home life and relationships and all of that, and work is crap, it's a bit easier to balance. It's still a thing, but it's a bit easier to balance, but what we know is that many people have a shit work life and a shit home life.

Dr. Dave:

Oh yeah.

Tracy:

Right, and that is a lot.

Dr. Dave:

Well, if they're not getting the goodness that they need, which is the language of belonging, this tone of invitation, this voice of acceptance, and the sounds of empathy that we need just to sustain ourselves

Tracy:

And, compassion from others, for yourself ... And, I think you talked about this, the levels of what those things are. Pity, something, empathy, and then compassion.

Dr. Dave:

Yeah, because it goes from pity, I feel sorry for you; to sympathy, I feel for you; to empathy, I feel with you; then compassion, I am here to help; and really walking through those levels of understanding the experience and how we could support each other, knowing which, I would say, emotions or actions, behaviors to introduce at this time for support.

Tracy:
And, I like support better than help, how can I support you, instead of I'm here to help because I think support ... Help, it's a different connotation. Like, "Oh, you think I need help?" That kind of thing for some people

Dr. Dave:
You're killing me, Tracy.

Tracy:
But support is however you want me to support you, I'm there.

Dr. Dave:
Now I need to change my mantra because my mantra is helping people to achieve their level of awesomeness. So, I need to change helping to supporting, man. Wow.

Tracy:
There you go.

Dr. Dave:
I'm in trouble. I even have it trademarked, so I need to go

Tracy:
Oh shit. No, you don't have to change that.

Dr. Dave:
I know I don't. I'm just thinking about it like, "Oh my God."

Tracy:
Oh shit, oh crap. No, it's just a different way to look at it. Help implies, I don't know, something else besides support for me.

Dr. Dave:
It's good stuff, but anything else you would like to talk about the language of belonging before we close out our convo for today?

Tracy:
No, I just really, really like this whole idea of belonging, and I think the more people define what that means for them, it may be easier to seek it out. And, I always want people to go with themselves first. If you feel like you can be your best friend and that you would like to be around a person like you, that's good. If you feel like, "Ugh, God, I wouldn't want to hang out with me. I'm a whole lot," if that's the thing, start working on loving yourself more and feeling like you belong to you, to who you are.

Dr. Dave:
Tracy, thank you so much. So hey, thank you for listening to the *KnolShare with Dr. Dave* podcast. Our conversation today was about the language of belonging. Look, language is important to feel a sense of connection and belonging to one's self. Belonging is a basic human need. It's an important part of who we are and how we could find identity, so I hope this learning experience prompted you to seek, to discover more ways of finding your level of awesomeness.

KnolShare with Dr. Dave Podcast is streamed in Spotify, iTunes, Audible, and Google Play.

I'm always going to give a shout out to my niece, Kayanna Brow-Hendrickson for dropping the music for this podcast.

This podcast is copywritten 2022 by Dr. Dave Cornelius and knolshare.org. Thank you for listening, and stay tuned for our next episode of belonging and healing as we continue to share our stories and experiences.

SENSE YOUR SPACE FOR BELONGING: A CONVERSATION WITH DR. DAVE AND TRACY TREACY

Podcast: *KnolShare with Dr. Dave*, found on Spotify, iTunes, Audible, and Google Play

VLog: https://vimeo.com/640754900

Dr. Dave:
So hello and welcome to the *KnolShare with Dr. Dave* podcast. This is Dr. Dave Cornelius, your host. I am super excited and pleased to announce the launch of a new series with my friend, Tracy Treacy. We're going to be talking about belonging and healing over several episodes, starting with one episode each month. We'll see where we go from there, right? Hey Tracy, what's going on?

Tracy:
Good morning, Dr. Dave. How are you?

Dr. Dave:
That's so formal. We know each other too long to be calling, well, you can call me Dr. Dave.

Tracy:
Well, I'm looking at your name on the screen and it says Dr. Dave, so I'm calling you Dr. Dave. Okay, I'll call you Cornelius. What's up, Cornelius? How you doing?

Dr. Dave:
I would rather you call me Dr. Dave. So, you know part of our conversation today, we have a few topics that we're going to go over. And since we're talking about belonging and so the four topics would be sensing our space for belonging, we'll probably dig into some generative workspace for belonging, don't fake belonging, and then back to your vision, get some ideas around how we could get there. So what do we want? So let's just jump in and let's talk about the importance of belonging for us human beings, right? I mean, this is something that we need. If we don't have it, we go stir crazy, I guess. Or we go and live in cabins out in the bush.

Tracy:
And some people like to do that because they belong out there, right, if you're talking about belonging. Yeah. You know, I was thinking about that belonging thing and what that means in the society that we live in, and how it's, you got to find your people in order to feel like you belong.

Dr. Dave:
Right.

Tracy:
Right. How do you find your people? And then when you find your people and you show up, do you feel like you're part of the people that you think you want to be a part of? So do you really feel like you belong?

Dr. Dave:
Yeah, that is a very insightful view, right, into those relationships, right, that you're trying to build with these individuals that you're part of. So, oftentimes we're looking in to see, hey, do they help us emotionally, right, do they make us happy or spiritually ...

Tracy:
Right.

Dr. Dave:
Or even from a physical context, right, are they helping us physically in terms of us being a part of their, that space, how do we sense that, right? Trying to figure that out.

Tracy:
Yeah, and do they make me happy or do they help me find my own happiness, when even in those groups of belonging, there's so much stuff that needs to be healed within those groups in order to feel like they even belong.

Dr. Dave:
Yeah.

Tracy:
I kind of think the sense of belonging comes back to self. Can I accept who I am and all of my stuff in order to show up authentically in a group that I think are my people, and then feel like I belong? And that was a whole lot, but that's kind of the trajectory, right?

Dr. Dave:
Yeah, because I think of it as self-love, self-respect, self-healing, right, self-esteem. I mean, it all comes, it starts with us because the sensing is from us into the environment with other people that we connect with, so it starts with us.

Tracy:
Yeah. I like using self-efficacy instead of self-esteem, right.

Dr. Dave:
Sure.

Tracy:
Because self-esteem feels to me more externally driven because I feel good when people respond to me in a certain kind of way, and it can also be internal, but I think, sometimes when we think self-esteem is how good do I feel about myself, and how good do I feel about myself when others are around. And sometimes we need the external environment to help us with that. When I think of self-efficacy is how do I feel about how I show up in what I know about myself, how efficient am I with Tracy, right? How do I know me? And I think it is a competency thing. How competent am I with myself? I think it's kind of a different take on that self-esteem thing.

Dr. Dave:
Well sure, efficacy definitely applies. And you know, how we feel about ourselves at times is driven by external sources, people, other people. But I think, when I think of happiness versus joy, right, those two different contexts, happiness is based on things that [have] happened or is happening. And joy is an internal, comes from the inside, so you have to have a balance of both for it to work really well for you to sense because, and I guess at some point you could not have any direction in a process of belonging, and then your sensing will take you in a different direction.

Tracy:
What do you mean? Give me more of that.

Dr. Dave:
Well, you have lots of people who may not have a sense of who they are.

Tracy:
I mean, the majority of people.

Dr. Dave:
Well, I can't say majority, I just say ...

Tracy:
I'm going to say majority.

Dr. Dave:
You say majority.

Tracy:
I'm going to say majority from the folks that I've worked with, majority of people were like, who am I, right?

Dr. Dave:
Yeah. And I think even more so now people are digging into that, who am I?

Tracy:
Mm-hmm [affirmative].

Dr. Dave:
Right. But, if we go beyond just the self, and I, sometimes I want to dig in to look at the past, right? And I think about Martin Luther King, Dr. Martin Luther King and his "I Have a Dream" speech, and as he was talking about society as a whole, and how the words of the Constitution kind of gave us this sense that we're heirs to the space that we live in, right? We're talking all people is what he was talking about, about life, liberty, and the pursuit of happiness, right. So, let's think about that from that context, and see where that leads us in this conversation.

Tracy:
Yeah, how? I get what you're saying, right? And I get that we're all heirs to whatever. And if we are looking at the past, right, the past is a lot of the, many of the, many of the situations I've seen, the past is the thing that creates the block for people actually feeling like they belong because there's so many hurts

from the past. And I don't mean as a people globally, I mean like personally, like my childhood kind of past and say much, can we cuss on here?

Dr. Dave:
You can do whatever.

Tracy:
Okay. It's, if my childhood was so fucked up that I can't, if it messed me up so much, I don't even know who I am, how am I going to find a sense of belonging? So I'm just kind of out here looking and searching in all these different places that may not be good for me, and I don't know if I'm going to ever belong. That's loneliness, right? That is just, that goes a whole another layer.

Dr. Dave:
That's deep, but I, and I tend to look at the, and this is my sense of optimism, right?

Tracy:
Right.

Dr. Dave:
I tend to look at the glass kind of half full. Because I think, there's a certain group of people out there who also, in spite of their upbringing and the challenges that they've experienced, they've been resilient enough to find a path forward, and be able to sense where they belong. And it takes time. It's not something that's going to be overnight, right, that's a lot of work. But what I was referring to was the Declaration of Independence, and falling heir to those wonderful words that we could embrace as part of who we are, that we have the rights to those things, those things are important for us.

Tracy:
Yeah.

Dr. Dave:
Even beyond just that document, how do we bring it into our life, that right for life, liberty, and the pursuit of happiness or pursuit of joy?

Tracy:
Yeah, I think that's what we're talking about, right?

Dr. Dave:
Yeah.

Tracy:
If we all have a right to that, how do we find that, how do we seek that out? And it, and my, I'm not saying the glass is not half full because it can still be half full and you can still do the work, the searching, and the seeking, and learn about the past, and discover who you are from that, and still feel joy. Those things can coexist together, right? So it's about the glass being half full and discovering what's in the other half of the glass.

Dr. Dave:
I completely agree, and a line on that, that yeah. You know, that is a thing, that is a reality, right, that's going to happen, that we're going to be half full and we still have to discover, I don't think we ever get to a point where, well, at least, let me just speak for me personally.

Tracy:
Yes.

Dr. Dave:
I'm always in discovery mode, and I'm seeking and acknowledging, and trying to get better as a human being every day. You know that's my journey, but that's just for me, most, I don't know, for some, that's not a thing: "I've reached where I've reached and that's good enough, leave me alone."

Tracy:
And that, that's why the world's so fun because there's so many different kinds of people, right?

Dr. Dave:
Yeah.

Tracy:
It's just, and so many walks of life, which takes us back to, you can find your place with some people, right? You can find your group, your fraternity, your brothers, your sisters, your people, you can find them.

Dr. Dave:
Yeah.

Tracy:
As you discover who you are, those things can happen together, they can coexist together. You don't have to discover who you are in order to feel like you belong. And you don't have to belong in order to discover who you are. Those things can work together.

Dr. Dave:
I agree. They, they're like your left and right hand working together, right? So I mean, as we say in the historical context, and you talk about your upbringing, right, and the impact of that, so I'm going to go to W. E. B. Dubois, and talk about his double consciousness that people of color sometimes have to experience, right, of we're in a code-switch mode, right? So, there's, when I'm with my people from the Virgin Islands, when I'm with African Americans from the United States, and when I'm with other people in my corporate setting, or even in the community that I live in, there's some double consciousness happening there, and some code-switching at times, right?

Tracy:

Yeah, and I think when W. E. B. Dubois said what he said, or Dubois, what he said, what he said, it was necessary for survival for people to code-switch, right? Because I think you said that was in 1903, that, and that was necessary. We're, even though we're 120 years later, people feel, still feel they need to code switch. And I guess I want to redefine this code-switching thing because I don't know if it serves us the way it, I don't know if it's necessary for us as a means of survival as it was in 1903, right? Because we could die in 1903, well, we could die today too.

Dr. Dave:

Yeah. Depends on where you are, man, where do you live?

Tracy:

Right, exactly. Right, exactly. However, in corporate America, when I think about code-switching, and then you going back to a black community and speaking differently, the words, the speaking is not necessarily the code-switch. That is just a vernacular; that is a colloquialism we move through when we move, talk to different people. My concern is when we code-switch is if we really change parts of ourself. That can get dangerous, and that leads to less belonging in a, in a community than anything. Even when you are with your people, because you got to recalibrate, when you get with your people, right? That's a lot; that's a heavy lift mentally. And that is exhausting for people. And I know many people still do that today, and they have to, they feel for survive. I want to start pushing back at that, I want to, I want, I want to, I want to, I want people to experiment to see how they show up in their authentic self when they're in spaces of people who are not their folk, and then see what that feels like and begin to kind of wear that and play with that.

Dr. Dave:
Well, yeah, because when we talk about our space of belonging, we want freedom from that double consciousness and that code-switching.

Tracy:
Right.

Dr. Dave:
And I mean that's, that's the end state, that's that end in mind that we want to get to, right, where we don't have to do that.

Tracy:
And we don't have to do it in those other spaces either, not only in our, and that's what I'm pushing back at.

Dr. Dave:
Yeah.

Tracy:
I want us to experiment with it when we're in those other spaces too, to just really be authentically you. And use it, and just show up as you and see what that feels like and how that's received, especially as the world is changing.

Dr. Dave:
Yeah. So I'll give you an example, like when I came to, when I went to college as a freshman, right? And I'm thinking about this code-switching, and this just came to mind.

Tracy:
Which was 80 years ago, but, okay, go ahead.

Dr. Dave:
Well fine, go ahead. And just throw me under the bus of 80 years ago, but here's the reality though. I think you were right there with me, weren't you?

Tracy:

Whatever. Keep going, keep moving. I'm not talking about code-switching. You are, go ahead.

Dr. Dave:

What I'm just giving you an example [of] is that growing up in the West Indies, we have a tendency to speak differently. Right. But, well, not a tendency. We do speak differently.

Tracy:

You do.

Dr. Dave:

And so I was in an English class and I was lectured to start working on my THS. Right. Cause you know, "deer, deer, and deer" means "there, there, and there." Right. You know? And so I'm talking about three different things, but where I come from is deer, deer, and deer. Right. So that was that level of coming into a society that they didn't understand my language. And I've had to learn how to code-switch and be mindful when I'm speaking of things, because sometimes I would say things like "plug it in and plug it out," instead of unplug it and plug it. And so what, what do you mean by plug it in? What do you, or plug it out? But that's the thing though, when I grew up with, we say things sometimes differently and I—

Tracy:

I totally get that. 'Cause I actually grew up in a household, said plug it in and plug it out.

Dr. Dave:

Okay. So I think it's a black people thing.

Tracy:

Maybe right. Maybe I don't know. And I get that and that, I guess that's part of it, not throwing you under the bus, but that was 40 years ago where you were an undergrad. Right?

Dr. Dave:
I don't think it was that long, but was close enough.

Tracy:
Okay whatever, when you started undergrad.

Dr. Dave:
Close enough, when I started undergrad, it was close enough.

Tracy:
Right. And I guess that's part of the point. For somebody who has some cultural humility. Some, I was a professor right. Professor for 20-some years, and I've had students from other countries speak in their country's colloquialism. I had to get used to it. I didn't want them to change how they showed up. I had to understand how they showed up.

Dr. Dave:
I think you are in a more informed space on than the other side. So that's a different—

Tracy:
—but I created that space and that's what I'm saying. I think people need to create those spaces so that we can feel like we belong and we don't have to change who we are.

Dr. Dave:
And I totally agree. I totally agree. And just things that we have to, not just, when I say we I'm talking about those of us who are either in a position in those position of powers as a professor, as a business leader. We have to create those spaces.

Tracy:
Position as yeah. All of those people. Right, right. absolutely.

Dr. Dave:
But also there's going to be some transition that you have to make in order for communication to be effective. And so my

friend from, all my friend from he is from New York, he goes, "Yeah, Mary, Mary, Mary." I'm like what? Yeah. It's just an East Coast thing. Right. That he talks about that in terms of Mary, merry—

Tracy:
Mary, Merry, and Marry.

Dr. Dave:
And Marry. Yeah. And he said, "Mary, Merry, Marry." He said, "That's just the way we talked." So got it. Yeah.

Tracy:
And then and when he said that, and maybe he was a white male, right. He was right. And that white male was saying, "Ye I'm not changing how I say, Mary, marry, or merry, you got to figure out what I'm saying." right? And they're expecting us to change things so they can understand us. And I say, they, when I'm talking people of power who may be white. And that to me is a double standard because this white dude is not, is going to say, "You have to accept how I say what I say. Yet, I'm not going to accept how you say what you say. Because you got to say it so I can understand it." I kind of think that's below cocky well.

Dr. Dave:
Yes, it's totally poppycock. It is.

Tracy:
And that's why I push back on code-switching because I think it's bullshit. Yeah. That's just me.

Dr. Dave:
And it's OK. Because you were just you Miss Tray-Tray. Cause it's just you.

Tracy:
Yeah. Yeah. So yeah, I think we can maybe think about that a little bit and people become more, a little more culturally. When I think about the cultural differences and nuances, we aren't going to know all of them. But I think it's okay to have a space where they're all welcome.

Dr. Dave:
Yes. Of course. We have to have a big enough tent or big enough space.

Tracy:
—and that's about belonging. Right. And that means you belong. Yeah. Okay. Yes. Yeah.

Dr. Dave:
Yeah. So in order for us to sense belonging, I believe we have to start with an end in mind. We have to have something that we could look forward to some visioning around what that looks like to you. I mean—

Tracy:
To belong? What if you don't know? I mean, because when I think about belonging and I'm say I'm out here trying to figure out where I belong and in what space I belong in, how am I going to know what that end goal is? If I don't even know where I'm going?

Dr. Dave:
There are two different things. The vision is one thing. And there's the experiments that you have to run to really figure this out. So there are two things happening. So you could have a vision, and the vision isn't static. Right? I mean our lives aren't static. I mean, I could create a vision for my life in a certain period of time. Right. And run through those experiments. They're like, okay. None of those things don't apply, take one.

Then go on to another period. So that's what we're talking about. We're not talking about being the end in mind being a static thing. Right. That it's a vision and visions do change. Yeah. So what does that look like? What would that look like? I mean, in terms of—

Tracy:
I don't know, to what, like have a vision, to have a goal?

Dr. Dave:
To have a vision. I'm talking about visions. What does that end kind of look like for whatever period of time it is?

Tracy:
Yeah. I guess that's just asking the person. So what do you want to be in three months? Where do you want to be in six, where do you want to be in a year? What do you want your life to look like? And then what are you, what are those steps toward that? If that's the thing and ... Go ahead.

Dr. Dave:
Beyond, beyond, beyond the clinical space, you, I'll, I'm just thinking of certain people that I've met in my life. That they've had a vision and you see it come to fruition. You watch them go through the experiments, and some of it may have been well planned. Some of it may not have been well planned. It has been a journey, but they still had a vision and I'm going to pull something in if this is okay.

Tracy:
You're going to do it anyway.

Dr. Dave:
And you know, I'm going to do it. So I'm thinking about your son when for the first time I met him and I, and I have a picture with him with a drumstick in his hand. And I think he was

just months old. I had this vision and what made me, not his vision, that he was going to be a drummer, which how weird is that? And that has come a thing. And I think he has had that vision throughout his life about being just that. Right. Without having a regimented plan, but he had a vision, right? Yeah.

Tracy:
Yeah, yeah. He was drumming while he was in my stomach. That boy beating on the drums. Right. He was like, da, da, da very chill, but just tapping, tapping, tapping, and tapping. Yeah. I guess because his vision was to be a touring musician. He knew that's what he wanted to do. So even mine, when I was six, I told my father, I was going to, when I grew up, I was going to be a shrink. Who the hell knows about a shrink at six years old. Right?

Dr. Dave:
You did.

Tracy:
Apparently. Right. So I don't know what I was watching on TV. I don't know what was going on, but that was the vi—didn't know how I was going to get there, but knew that that was a thing. And I don't know if that's more intuitive, if that's like your, I mean, this can go a whole nother way. Is that like your soul talking to you and you're listening and you're tapped in or is it just arbitrary?

Dr. Dave:
I don't know. I know that I wasn't that young, but I was in 11th grade, 80 years ago. And I knew that I wanted to study computer science. Have never seen a computer a day in my life, but that's what I wanted to do. And you know what the trigger was? It wasn't about computers. The trigger was about the possibility of being able to create music and do all of these

other things that I have passion about that I could do it with this medium. And I'm going to like, "Wow, that's cool. Imagine if I could do music," and 80 years ago, I'm poking fun at you.

Tracy:
I know you are. I know you're—

Dr. Dave:
With your ageism stuff. Young one.

Tracy:
If the age fits.

Dr. Dave:
It does.

Tracy:
I get that. I get that. And maybe people have that vision when they're young. And it's that question? What did you want to be when you grow up? Right? And then they think first thing, and sometimes kids, or adults will rattle off when they were children. Well, first it was a firefighter, then it was an astronaut. Then it was this. And it was that. And then they realized when that shifted, they're like, "Oh, but in high school, there was this teacher that recognized something that I was good at. And I knew that's what I wanted to do."

Dr. Dave:
Well, and then also it's those things that you rattle off is what Mom and Dad said, right? Mom and Dad said, or even people in your community, "You should aspire to be this." Versus what that vision is that you would have, so that you may find your sense of belonging [in] that space, right? Because that's an important thing to have a space of belonging.

Tracy:
Right. Right. And that goes, I mean, we can talk about culture with that too, because certain cultures may not allow for their kids to dream in those non-creative or those creative spaces, it's doctor, lawyer, you know, those kind of jobs go where the money is, computer science that kind of stuff. And then how do, how do we, how do those people find that sense of belonging if they've been directed culturally to do a certain thing?

Dr. Dave:
Yep. Yep. That's a very interesting thing. Yeah. But if we ... So can we pursue a generative workspace of belonging? Right. And when I'm thinking of generative is it's the whole aspect of being, giving birth to new ideas of who you are and where you want to be, who you want to be within the place that you work. Right? Whether that's in your own home office or at somewhat corporate office or at a client space. What does that look like for you? I know it's a big, big, chunky conversation that we could have.

Tracy:
Yeah. It's chunky because, I mean, full disclosure, I've never worked for anybody. I've worked in the, I know, right? I was a professor, so I worked in the university system. Right? But you don't really work. You work for university, but there's not, there's nobody looking at my curriculum or lesson plans or whether, I mean, I submit it. It's okayed. And then I teach my class. Right? And I've always been in private practice as a clinician, and I've had my own facilities and clinics where I could help people. So I can talk in context when my, when people are like, "Hey, Tracy, I want to start this new program. I think we could do this or that." And the other, if we're talking about the work environment, supporting that generative growth or belonging, that's about saying, "Okay, give me a

plan. How you going to do it? How you going to execute it? What's it going to cost us?" All of the things that I would need in order to say, "Let's do it now," or "Let's table it." But I think there should be an environment created so that can happen. Right.

Dr. Dave:
And I would agree. And maybe it doesn't need to be that overly structured: that it's a space that we could experiment. And I, and we call limited experiments where "yes,

let's try that and see how that works." And if it does, and everyone adds value to everyone, then maybe that's the thing that we adopt and we start practicing.

Tracy:
Yeah, how do you do that if you're a person that has never done that for themselves? And how do you, if you're at an employer, how do you set a space for your employees to be able to do that?

Dr. Dave:
Well, a fun way of doing that is you could use simple things of gamification, right? I mean, we use this concept of open space.

Tracy:
Okay.

Dr. Dave:
Where anyone could bring an idea and we could explore that idea, and then we could agree if that's something that we want to do as a collective. Right? So you may have the idea that, "Hey, I could wear my hair any way I want to without you having to judge me based on the hairstyle that I have. Can we explore that? And can we have conversations around that?" And all these are simple techniques that ...

Tracy:
Right.

Dr. Dave:
It wasn't born in corporate America, just to let you know. The whole open space technology stuff came from West Africa.

Tracy:
Okay. Yep.

Dr. Dave:
Where people in the tribe would come together and they would bring their challenges to the circle of individuals, and they'll have conversations about it, then they'll say, "Well, what do we all think? Right? Okay, yeah, yeah. Okay. Let's go do that."

Tracy:
Mm-hmm [affirmative].

Dr. Dave:
And you may have to come back again and say, "You know, we tried it, but it didn't really work."

Tracy:
Yeah.

Dr. Dave:
They're still taking out my goat milk. I'm just being facetious about that.

Tracy:
No, no, no, no. I know. But that's all community supported, right? That is a ... That sounds like grassroots. That sounds like community organization that ... I guess my question and this, and I don't know, it's not like we're going to answer it, but this is a question that I have.

Dr. Dave:
Yeah.

Tracy:
How is that space created if there is a leader that does not encourage that thinking? That's the thing. So I guess that leader, if they trust the people around them to carry things out and they don't do it. But some ... I just think of certain leaders we've had that have a very certain way of thinking, right?

Dr. Dave:
Yeah, yeah.

Tracy:
And there is no room for expansion. There is no room for that creativity.

Dr. Dave:
Well, the thing is, it's not always just about the will of that leader, right? It could also be about the will of the people in a grassroot fashion running their experiments, right?

Tracy:
Right.

Dr. Dave:
I mean, not everything starts from the top ...

Tracy:
Right.

Dr. Dave:
And trickles down to the bottom, right? We have things that start in a grassroot level. Many things in our country or in the world started at a grassroots level where people found a need, they ran their experiment, and then it came up where it became widely accepted. So, I think it's the same principle of creating. I think you need to have people who are willing to take that risk.

Tracy:
Right, and I guess I'm just thinking of it in a company context. I get that on a global, worldly context, but I'm thinking of a company context. And you got the male person and the assistant and this that want to do something different to make the systems better, but it's got to trickle up instead of down, and who's going to listen to it? And that's, yeah. That's where I get by.

Dr. Dave:
Yeah, it takes work. And there's been many successes where those individuals in those roles have created new ideas that have made companies very profitable, right? And make individuals find their sense of belonging in a new concept or new business idea.

Tracy:
Yeah, I would like for those things to be more public so that we know this is happening. So that people in these companies can feel like they can do that.

Dr. Dave:
Yeah.

Tracy:
Yeah.

Dr. Dave:
You hear about these things in TED talks.

Tracy:
Right, right, right. Right.

Dr. Dave:
This is where you hear about them after the fact ...

Tracy:
Right, right.

Dr. Dave:

Because the oppressive leader, the narcissistic leader, is not going to want to put that out there in public, yeah.

Tracy:

Right, right. So, yeah. I guess you call it the little guy, but it's not the little guy, it's the foundation of the business, right?

Dr. Dave:

Yeah.

Tracy:

It's those pillars in the business that make a big difference sometimes.

Dr. Dave:

Yeah, yeah. And I ... Little guys is just pecking order, right? The hierarchy.

Tracy:

Right, right. And that gives them a sense of belonging. Like, "Yeah, I belong to this company. Look at what I've contributed." And that's empowering. That is, I think, is golden. And you can take that sense of empowerment from work, and that can translate to so many other areas in your life.

Dr. Dave:

Of course.

Tracy:

For self-efficacy, right?

Dr. Dave:

Yeah, yeah.

Tracy:

That confidence, yeah.

Dr. Dave:
Yeah, that's self-love and self-respect, stuff that's so important, you know? But one thing I would like to say is that we shouldn't fake it. If belonging isn't working, is that don't fake it until you make it? If that's a thing, and I know many people have done that, I mean I have, and it's been harmful to me.

Tracy:
How do you ... Right, right. I was going to say, how do you fake belonging without harming yourself, right?

Dr. Dave:
Well, you do harm yourself. That's a fact, right? So the thing is, how do we get people to be as authentic as they possibly can? Or at least go through that journey, because that is hard stuff, right? Because the common position is we fall right back in with double consciousness and code-switching too, right? It's like, "Oh my God. In order for us to survive here, I have to dress a certain way. I have to speak a certain way. I have to have certain mannerisms. I have to like golfing or to drink a lot." And as we start to think about these different things that other people get involved with, oftentimes we're faking into that space so that we can have a sense of belonging, which is not healthy. We know that, right?

Tracy:
Mm-hmm [affirmative], mm-hmm [affirmative].

Dr. Dave:
So.

Tracy:
And I guess we have to define what do we want to belong to?

Dr. Dave:
Yes.

Tracy:

And where do we want to belong? And I guess that goes back to the beginning of the conversation. How the hell do you find that when you are not ... And I'm going to go back to childhood, I guess. If you're not somebody in your home as a kid being asked those questions or even honoring that you feel a certain kind of way about doing a certain kind of thing, right? Even like eating food. And this is from ... This is a cultural standpoint. And so I'm sure other cultures do that, but "if this is what I cook for dinner, and you ain't eating it, you're going to starve." Right? Even that kind of thing is like ... The parent ain't got time, for one. I totally get that. And can't be feeding five or six different palates if you don't want to eat it. Totally get that.

There could be a dialogue, though. "Okay, what don't you like about this? Maybe we could plan the meals on the weekend and somebody gets something they like every night." There's so many other negotiating tools. And if that isn't done in a household where that's a norm, how is a person going to know how to do that as an adult?

Dr. Dave:

You know, as you speak of that, I think of my own childhood. At a very young age, I decided that I wanted to be a vegetarian. I think it was in fifth grade.

Tracy:

Okay.

Dr. Dave:

And I think because my mother had the experience of her mother being a vegetarian.

Tracy:

Okay.

Dr. Dave:
It made it a lot easier for her to be considerate, creating space, and said, "Okay, you want to do this?"

Tracy:
Mm-hmm [affirmative].

Dr. Dave:
"I am going to make things without meat for you. And I'm going to help you to learn how to eat this way so that you don't die of scurvy."

Tracy:
Yeah. Right. But how wonderful is that, right?

Dr. Dave:
That's what I'm saying.

Tracy:
Yeah.

Dr. Dave:
That was an amazing experience. So I didn't have to fake belonging because I looked at other kids that I grew up with.

Tracy:
Yep.

Dr. Dave:
And I could just remember these girls and their mom. And their mother slaughtered a pig, or their family slaughtered a pig, and they had the pig head there. And the mother is like, "You got to eat that there! You eat the eyes! Eat the feet!" And she's like, "Mommy, the eyes are looking at me." And I'm like ... Every time I ... That is imprinted in my mind.

Tracy:
Yeah.

Dr. Dave:
And that was really, really young when that happened.

Tracy:
Yeah, yep.

Dr. Dave:
But that is ...

Tracy:
Yeah, that's a great example.

Dr. Dave:
Yeah.

Tracy:
That's a great example of that. And food I was using because many of us can relate to that.

Dr. Dave:
Yeah.

Tracy:
But when we talk about feelings and emotions, or even having a voice ...

Dr. Dave:
Yeah.

Tracy:
I mean think about how we're ... Our generation, children are to be seen and not heard. Right? And as soon as a child speaks, it's like, "Don't talk back."

Dr. Dave:
Yep.

Tracy:
"Don't give me lip." And all that kid is doing is voicing what they feel.

Dr. Dave:
Yeah.

Tracy:
So they get the message that that's not good. So how do I even get that sense of that framework you're talking about of that authenticity? How can I show up authentic when, when I have shown up authentic, it has gotten me in trouble? So I'm going to really learn how to be a chameleon.

Dr. Dave:
Yeah.

Tracy:
And that's the code-switching part, right? I'm going to learn how to be able to fit in any kind of group, or I'm going to learn how to get in the background where nobody really sees me. I'm going to be smaller than I want to be so that I'm not drawing attention to myself. That, I don't know. It just gives that sense of not belonging more weight. Right?

Dr. Dave:
Yeah, it's the work. I mean, there's a serious amount of work that takes place to actually find that place of belonging. And yes, it could start from our childhood, right?

Tracy:
Yeah.

Dr. Dave:
Where we've been given permission to behave in certain ways. And it's not "yackety-yak, don't talk back, here's a smack," right?

Tracy:
Right.

Dr. Dave:
Which is some people's experiences.

Tracy:
Right.

Dr. Dave:
And others where we have the opportunity to go into, "Hey, Mom, I want to be vegetarian. Is that okay?" And Grandma. And great manipulation, right? "Grandma has been a vegetarian for a long time."

Tracy:
Right.

Dr. Dave:
"And I want to follow in her footsteps." So, at least I had cover, I had Grandma.

Tracy:
Mm-hmm [affirmative], mm-hmm [affirmative].

Dr. Dave:
And so, there's just a lot of work when it comes into trying to be your authentic self in a space where you could belong, right?

Tracy:
Yeah, when I think of authentic self ... So I've been trained in so many different areas, and trauma comes to mind with authentic self, right?

Dr. Dave:
Mm-hmm [affirmative].

Tracy:
Trauma, shame, those kinds of things. And what I understand about authentic self ... There's this theory, or there are these

many theories, one particular is called parts, that we all have parts to ourselves.

Dr. Dave:
Yes.

Tracy:
And those parts are developed in order to survive situations. I think when we have to, the more parts we build within, the more the authentic self gets covered up. And those parts may need to be ... That's where the work comes in. Those parts are there for safety. They're there for a reason, but sometimes they are so active, that they cover up who I really am.

Dr. Dave:
And that's true because what is developed out of that is what we call limiting beliefs, right?

Tracy:
Right.

Dr. Dave:
And so those limiting beliefs are those things that, "I don't, I can't do that. I'm not good enough. I have to be this way, otherwise, I won't fit." And those are all limiting beliefs. And those are those things that are attached to the parts and areas that we create in our lives in order for us to survive in these spaces.

Tracy:
Mm-hmm [affirmative]. And sometimes that's just one part.

Dr. Dave:
Yeah.

Tracy:
That one part can be so loud that, "I can't do that. I'm not smart enough for that."

Dr. Dave:
And it's always the loudest part, right?

Tracy:
Right, it's the loudest part. So if it's so loud, how are you, your authenticity ever going to come out? It's about ... And it's not even about turning down the volume. It's about talking to that part because when that part pops up, I bet the person is really scared in those situations. Right? And then that part pops up for them to be safe. And then I think you need to communicate with that part and be like, "Okay part, let's do this thing. I can be scared and still do."

Dr. Dave:
Yeah.

Tracy:
Right. And that goes back to what we were talking about. All those things can be both, and I can be authentic, and I can be scared to do that.

Dr. Dave:
Well, as I'm drawing on my experience as you're talking about that, I went to work for a very large organization back then. They were like the top six accounting auditing company in the world. And got to work for one of those companies, and I just remember going out to lunch one of departments. This is one of the things that the experience that you, you had, right, of faking where you belong, and all of the servers were black people wearing white gloves. I had never seen anything like that before in my life. On TV, yes.

Tracy:
Right.

Dr. Dave:
But that was just such a weird ... I felt so weird being there and felt like, "God, I'm like so out ..." I wanted to run out of that space. But I knew I couldn't run because this was an important aspect of this career journey I was on in corporate America.

Tracy:
Okay.

Dr. Dave:
And I don't know, man, I ... They think about that job of how much I had to fake to belong.

Tracy:
Yes.

Dr. Dave:
Right, every day. The way we dressed, the way we spoke, and one voice, one look; there was these regimented things in that period of time that ... And it wasn't just me.

Tracy:
Right.

Dr. Dave:
The deal coming from a different culture. I mean, I remember this one woman just having a nervous breakdown, trying to belong, and we were there like late night one night, and she was standing on her desk screaming at the top of her ... She was having a nervous breakdown; we had to call 9-1-1.

So, I mean, just imagine her as a white woman, I'm a black man. Just dealing with, "Oh God, how do we fit into this space that was created by this patriarchal model of where we have to fake to belong?"

Tracy:
The ... And this is just such an aside, but when you say nervous breakdown, I know that's a common colloquialism for our society to express when someone can't handle anything anymore. I don't call those a nervous breakdown, I call those breakthroughs because that—

Dr. Dave:
That's a very positive way.

Tracy:
Yes. She could not take any more. So she was like, "If I take anymore, I'm going to fucking explode." And she did—

Dr. Dave:
Well, she did—

Tracy:
To let it out. Yes, she had to let it out, and the thing after that though is calming her nervous system and making sure she's okay.

Dr. Dave:
Yes.

Tracy:
And not looking at it as a negative. But if some ... I pray to God, for those of us who believe in God, the Universe, Spirit. I pray to Spirit that somebody afterwards said to that woman, "Thank you for doing that; now let's see what you want to do."

Dr. Dave:
Not in that era.

Tracy:
I know.

Dr. Dave:
No.

Tracy:
I know.

Dr. Dave:
She didn't last very long, just to let you know. I remember her coming back to work and seeing that she was in a totally different space.

Tracy:
She was medicated, that's why.

Dr. Dave:
Yes. She was ... It's like this person come in and going like, "Oh my gosh, wow!"

Tracy:
Right, and all that passion and all that creativity was like, "Eh", locked in. Yes, I call that a breakthrough, but I know ... And that to me sounds like a very, very hard situation that many people go through. In particular ... Not necessarily just in corporate America, just working in spaces that are very patriarchal driven, are very mono view of the world. That is a very difficult thing and that wreaks havoc on your physical health, mental health, emotional health, psycho ... All the health, all the health. All of them.

Dr. Dave:
All those parts that are essential for you to function in a healthy way. I mean, it's my God ... Blows my mind.

Tracy:
Yes.

Dr. Dave:
So we're talking about, "How do we come up with vision?", and here I am jumping to a visioning journey map, a little thing that I like to play with, which has been helpful for and for some of my clients where I said, "Start with the end in mind; it does not have

to be perfect. I want to just make sure that there's no perfectionist, and then let's envision what it's like if we went out three, six months, and you wanted to walk back from your vision, what are all the hurdles that you think you may run into?"

And you come back to your current day and then you go forward and said, "Well, what are all the things? What are all the goals? What are all the things that I want to dream about until I get to that vision?" And you start collecting and writing those down. So this is a simple tool that I have used to work with different people. And then there's a bunch of questions that I want to ask around why we're going through that journey. It's almost like a journey mapping; we want to go through and figure out, "What does this look like?" because there's no perfection in this.

Tracy:
Right.

Dr. Dave:
We know that we're going to fail; we know we're going to have some successes and we're going to have breakthroughs and discovery in the process. So that's a whole thing about when I think about creating visions that, they're not static, they're not monuments, that we're ... on the mall in Washington looking at.

Tracy:
Right.

Dr. Dave:
What are your thoughts around those type of tools like this that would help people just see things? To me, it's amazing sometimes when I could get up and put a sticky in a wall. Like, "Hey, here's a sticky with something that's really important on it or a picture." And that also sometimes gets people insights, "Oh, wow. That's possible."

Tracy:
Yes, that's a big intersection. I think of how we could both approach something in a similar way because the end is maybe necessary for some people. Whatever that end is. And I think if, when I'm working with people, if there is say, "I want," hell a big one, "I want to lose weight."

I swear, my question ... And you have many questions along the way. So you do a timeline and I guess within what you're saying, I agree with all of it. The three month and the six month thing down the road, I don't know if I ... It's good to say.

Dr. Dave:
Yes.

Tracy:
It's good to have just a benchmark and to have flexibility within that benchmark. Even if you say something now and we meet in two or three weeks and you don't reach that benchmark, let's recalibrate. That's okay. There's a lot of false starts.

It takes the average person seven times to go through rehab in order to handle whatever that addiction is. And when I say handle, it may mean abstinence for some, it may mean harm reduction for others, whatever it is for that person. So it's not going to just happen the first time, so I think those mini baby steps ... That's what you're sounding like to me.

Dr. Dave:
It's incremental stuff right?

Tracy:
Incremental step, right. The, the little baby goals to get through and then the big picture starts to form more and more and more.

Dr. Dave:
That's true and, and as you're going through there, what we're looking at is what type of questions could we ask? 'Cause it's not just, "Oh, I'm going to look at hurdles." So it could say,

"Well, when facing these hurdles, who do I need to be in this, at that moment?" And whether it's losing weight or a career or building a relationship, "Who do I need to be?"

And that's also the sense of belonging or maybe it's my perspective on the world. "How does that limit me in this process?" So as we are going through the journey, there's a series of questions that we want to just prompt ourselves in the process so we could learn more because it's a discovery, it's an experiment.

Tracy:
It's a journey. Life is a journey, and I think those questions change, and how we get to how we do what we do changes, and it's really important in parts of this to ask people: where have they felt like they've succeeded and what took them ... What parts of them were used in order for that success and to be able to transfer those skills to this new thing?

Because we know they can do it, and we know there's the capability and there's the confidence in all of that. And then that's where I see people go, "Yeah I can do great with other people in other situations, but with this one, I seem to just lose my shit."

Dr. Dave:
Yes. And look man, it's really important for us to have grace with ourselves. That's part of empathy for ourselves, as well as we're going through this journey of trying to understand—

Tracy:
I think self-compassion is so important.

Dr. Dave:
Yes.

Tracy:
So very important.

Dr. Dave:
Yes, it is. Things that we have to do. So I think this is ... What do you think, this is a good time for us to bring this to close? I think we have some great conversation happening. Anything that you would like to add before we jump out until our next episode?

Tracy:
No, this was kind of fun; we don't know where it's going. We're kind of on a journey ourselves. We've ... To see how this works out. How whatever ... Our end goal is to continue to do podcasts.

Dr. Dave:
Yes, right!

Tracy:
Right.

Dr. Dave:
It's an experiment.

Tracy:
It's an experiment. No, I think we're good.

Dr. Dave:
Good. So, well, hey, thank you for listening to the *KnolShare with Dr. Dave* podcast, with my friend Tracy Treacy and as we're on this journey, talking about belonging and healing as part of our process and journey. And I'd just like to say, this is copywritten 2021, Dr. Dave Cornelius on KnolShare.org. And we look forward to speaking to you next time. So we'll probably set up a few different ways that you could connect with us as we post our podcast, and thank you so much, Tracy, for going on this venture with me.

THE ROOT BEFORE THE FRUIT: A CONVERSATION WITH DR. DAVE AND TRACY TREACY

Podcast: *KnolShare with Dr. Dave,* found on Spotify, iTunes, Audible, and Google Play

VLog: https://vimeo.com/685017609

Dr. Dave:
So hello and welcome to the *KnolShare with Dr. Dave* podcast. This is Dr. Dave Cornelius, your host. We're continuing the conversation of belonging and healing with my guest, Tracy Treacy from D & S Healing Center. Hey Tracy Treacy, how have you been?

Tracy:
Woo-hoo. Awesome. I've been doing well. How about you, sir?

Dr. Dave:
You know, same here, same here. Just one day at a time. We use the metaphor, an island of one, one, one, one. It's like walking, so one, one.

Tracy:
Okay.

Dr. Dave:
Okay. Yeah. Hey, we're getting into the conversation around healing. So one, one. One foot in front of the other because sometimes that's what it takes, right?

Tracy:
Yeah. I mean you don't want to go backwards, though sometimes you do, but the idea is to ... one foot in front of the other to keep it moving. Yeah.

Dr. Dave:
Yeah. You got to keep it moving.

Tracy:
I guess I didn't get the island reference with that and—

Dr. Dave:
Yeah.

Tracy:
... but you islanders got your way of doing things.

Dr. Dave:
Yeah. Well, that's what I learned. It's a thing.

Tracy:
It's a thing. One, one, here we go.

Dr. Dave:
One one. So here's a quote, a couple quotes that I grabbed from Vienna Pharaon. And her name is, "Healing happens when you move through the pains, the patterns, and stories, and walk your way into a healthy ending." And that's one quote, and then, Maya Angelou of course, she says, "Forgive yourself for not knowing what you didn't know before you learned it." So our conversation today is the root before the fruit. So the root before the fruit concept describes the need for solid root to support a sustainable opportunity to bear fruit in our healing space. Right? And so we're going to ... I'm using I, I'm using the metaphor of sower who owns good soil to plant seeds. And good soil is rich with nutrients, which created space for plants and to have an abundant food supply to support healthy

development. And I'm just using us, our bodies, our minds, our spirit, as that soil. And the work that we go through ... the healing aspect is the seed. So good seeds are also essential for the process of growing healthy fruits. So you are a sower, aren't you?

Tracy:
I would say yes. I have not heard that term, but I'm going to say yes.

Dr. Dave:
So tell me, let's talk about you as a sower.

Tracy:
You know—

Dr. Dave:
I know you're doing some good stuff.

Tracy:
Well, I mean, I do call myself a healer. Right?

Dr. Dave:
Okay. There you go.

Tracy:
And my healing can only happen when I'm co-creating that space for a person ... I'm creating a space for a person to help them heal, which is the co-creation. Right? That's with us working together and me supporting that work. And there are many different ways to do the work. I find the richest way to do the work is through the body. Right? And then that combines ... the body, I don't think of separate as the mind. I think of that altogether. There's this one theory ... oh my gosh, Dave, I can't remember who said it. I want to say it goes back to Freud, of how the neck is the separator. No, it goes back to Jung, not Freud. How the neck is a separator from the mind and the

body. And that what we do is we cut off. We, we become very heady.

We become a world, a society, a community that really values the intellect. And then what the body holds is the feelings. And it holds the experiences. And we don't want that to interfere with how things are processed up here, but there's no way we can't have that thing work. And I think the neck is the thing that connects the mind and body. You know, con-neck? I call it a con-neck.

Dr. Dave:
Yeah.

Tracy:
Right?

Dr. Dave:
Yeah, yeah.

Tracy:
I spell it C and then E-C-K. The c-eck-ter. Right? The mind and the body. Because it does connect the two. So, I mean, when I say the body, I say mind and body, and I think we're all spirit, we come from spirit. So to me, that's all combined. The mind, body, and the spirit. They're not separate. And for us to approach healing as in separating those spaces, it makes it more difficult to forgive. It makes it more difficult to ... as the first quote, healing happens when you move through the pain, the patterns, and the stories. I know when a person has worked through their stuff is when their bodies no longer have a response to that thing. Because now the body is healed.

Dr. Dave:
Yeah. Well, you can see it in their faces, on the body languages, right? Or even just the thought of an individual or a certain situation. You see you shift—

Tracy:
Yeah.

Dr. Dave:
... in that human being, right? That person kind of like, "Whoa. Hey, come on now." So ...

Tracy:
Well, I mean, I believe there's this thing called the pain body. So what we can see is how a person carries their trauma. And I've gotten really good at people, just looking at people, not necessarily knowing what their trauma is, but knowing that there has been trauma by the way they walk and present and move. And the body tells ... we'll talk about some things later, but there's this book called *The Body Keeps the Score*. So the body keeps all of the memories. Right? That it should have stored on a cellular level. So we've got to release it cellularly.

Dr. Dave:
Certainly, certainly. So, when I think of healing, I think there's three different aspects, even though it's one. There's one person, right? I think that there's a psychological aspect of healing. Right? There's a physical which [is] somatic. Right? But also there's a spiritual aspect of it. So I think all three are needed for us to really come full circle, with dealing with whatever trauma or pain that's been introduced into our lives either by ourselves or by someone else.

Tracy:
Right.

Dr. Dave:
Right?

Tracy:
Right.

Dr. Dave:
So if we had to start with the psychological aspect of it, what are your thoughts of how that works? And how that has been working in terms of a healing tool? As a seed for healing?

Tracy:
Yeah. So what psychology has done with healing and pain is we've made it clinical.

Dr. Dave:
Right.

Tracy:
And so we have a diagnosis for things. And—

Dr. Dave:
"You're crazy."

Tracy:
Well, that is not a clinical diagnosis. However, that's what people call folks who have a clinical diagnosis. Right? So say you have a clinical diagnosis of ... I'm going to say bipolar disorder. And this is a very con— I'm saying something very controversial, but I'm just going to do it. Okay?

Dr. Dave:
Yeah.

Tracy:
Bipolar disorder can be a chemical imbalance, right? And that's how it's diagnosed. So you get drugs, medications, things to help with the bipolar disorder because those are ups and downs in moods. Which is great. Right? Because some people may go that route with the medications, and some people may not go that route. That is a personal choice. I think what we have forgotten, and what is now beginning to happen ... so I'm talking about old psychology, old social work. We never

thought about trauma in those diagnoses. And now we're becoming a more trauma-informed society, which is great.

So now we can bring that stuff into some of these diagnoses. So when I think about psychology, maybe there was a little bit of a clinical lean to it, and now there's becoming more of a trauma-informed care. Social work is doing a great job with that, and psychology is doing a great job as well. So I think across the board, we can talk about how trauma has affected our mental health, which is the psychology, right? Of how we do things and how we view the world.

So I think when we talk about, "Girl, you need to go to the therapist; you got some stuff that handled." That's the psychology. Right? And that is being able to speak with someone to help you through the pain and the traumas of what you've gone through in your life in a way that they can help you to understand that you are not your trauma. That trauma is an experience that you experienced, which may have caused you to move through the world a certain kind of way, and hopefully, the therapy psychology part of it can help you see that, and help heal those wounds and change the behavior that you developed from those wounds.

Dr. Dave:
Yes.

Tracy:
Does that make sense?

Dr. Dave:
That makes all the sense in the world, of how that practice can be used to help us really understand ourselves and the things that have happened to us.

Tracy:
Right.

Dr. Dave:

Right? And how can we heal from that? Sometimes, even some of those healing remedies, and I'm just calling them remedies, that they're going to be experienced differently. Right? Just based on the concept of if we're metabolizing that healing into our mind, body and spirit. So what happens when it doesn't work? Or it's not working well? Or it even had ... I'm asking more questions, or even has an adverse effect on the individual?

Tracy:

So that's a whole lot, what you just asked.

Dr. Dave:

I know. Well, I'm talking to you, so I'm expecting you to ... throw stuff at me, right?

Tracy:

Okay. Let's break that down.

Dr. Dave:

Let's unpack that. How's that?

Tracy:

Let's unpack that. So the idea is to not harm a person, or re-harm a person, or re-traumatize a person, as they go through healing. The goal is for them ... so when I think about trauma, and what I'd like to say to people and ... think of your life trauma or experiences as an observer, to try and detach from that serious physiological pain that it may give you. And begin to look at it as a story, not that you didn't go through it, but as you were going through it, how were you feeling? What was your body doing? How was your body responding? And then you can break down the levels of trauma or the stages of trauma. There's ... I learned ... it's called ITR. I learned ... gosh, I can't even think of the word. It's a process; it's a technique; it's a strategy. It's a healing modality. Right? And it is really breaking the trauma down into parts or sections. Telling a story within that section, rewriting that entire ... knowing that, that, story happened,

... and giving that story a finality, right? So there's the beginning, a middle, and end, right?

Dr. Dave:
Yep.

Tracy:
So we've got these aspects of this story. We've got ... I think I just went way off course, but here we go. Because you asked that question.

Dr. Dave:
It's not my fault.

Tracy:
You asked that question and here we go. So when we break down trauma, let's break it down into stages. So we've got a startle stage, like, "Oh shit, something's about to ..." You know how you walk through life and you think, "Things are going way too good. That shoe is about to drop."

Dr. Dave:
Yeah, oh boy. Yeah, we always get that mindset, like, "Something's about to happen."

Tracy:
Yep. "Things have been going too smooth. I know something's about to come down." Right?

Dr. Dave:
Right.

Tracy:
If our bodies are always in that anxious state, that's like a startle. It's like when babies get startled and they're like ... You got to brace yourself for that shit, right?

Dr. Dave:
Yeah. Yeah.

Tracy:
After you're startled, and then you go into this fight or flight, because you're like, "I got to get out of Dodge or I got to bulldoze this thing." Right? Sometimes we can't fight or flight, so what happens to a person is they freeze.

Dr. Dave:
Yep.

Tracy:
Right? So your body just goes ... and you freeze and you can shut down. Right? So when we're freeze, maybe we could call that depression or something, in a freeze state. Okay? When I'm frozen, I got this thing where, if I'm frozen, I really don't want to be here. I'm just going to check out of my reality. Right? So I'm going to dissociate.

Dr. Dave:
Yes.

Tracy:
And when people dissociate with trauma, some of us get stuck in the dissociation. Right? And we get really good at not feeling the feels. We get really good at not letting folks affect us. So we put up these walls so that we don't feel the stuff, and that's dissociating. And sometimes we can do that so well, we might get a diagnosis from that. We don't know what that is, but a diagnosis could come from that.

Dr. Dave:
Certainly.

Tracy:
So if I'm going through a traumatic event, I got the startle, this fight or flight, I got this freeze, I'm going to check out because I don't want to deal with the pain that I'm going through. But then something about the brain says, "You know what? You can't stay out here forever. So you're just going to obey and do what you need to do in order to live." Because sometimes we feel like we're going to die.

Dr. Dave:
Well, certainly. Yeah.

Tracy:
Right?

Dr. Dave:
As you were talking about that disassociation, I was thinking of Jeffrey Dahmer. I don't know why he came into mind, but—

Tracy:
I don't either, but tell me more about that.

Dr. Dave:
Well, I'm just thinking about, to be able to have someone for lunch or dinner, how much of a disassociation has to take place that you get to that place?

Tracy:
Yeah.

Dr. Dave:
Right.

Tracy:
Yeah, yeah.

Dr. Dave:
I mean ...

Tracy:
What a state that is.

Dr. Dave:
I don't remember if I was living in Wisconsin or Illinois at the time when that was taking place, but it kind of freaked me out a lot.

Tracy:
Mm-hmm [affirmative].

Dr. Dave:
You know?

Tracy:
Yeah. I mean, to hack up a body, to have body parts in your refrigerator, I mean, that takes a level of dissociation, right?

Dr. Dave:
Yeah.

Tracy:
Wow. Wow. It's that kid that is in the classroom, that they're daydreaming out the window or they're doing something and you're like, "Yo. Hey, are you here?" And you're like, "Hey, what? Yeah, I'm here." But they weren't, right?

Dr. Dave:
Yeah.

Tracy:
You don't know what's been going on at home so that they can do that. Right?

Dr. Dave:
Yeah, that's true. Yeah. Sorry.

Tracy:
So, that child feels, "Okay, I got to get out of this space." After they dissociate, then they have to automatically obey. Because if the teacher goes ... "Dave, stop daydreaming."

Dr. Dave:
Yeah. "Wake up."

Tracy:
"Come back here." And then, you're going to be like, "Okay, sorry," and you going to do what that teacher says, right?

Dr. Dave:
Mm-hmm [affirmative].

Tracy:
So that's automatic obedience. And that's what we do when we want to stay safe. We get into automatic obedience. After we take all that energy to do what we're supposed to do so we don't die, so we can survive, we got to do this thing called self-repair.

Dr. Dave:
Yeah.

Tracy:
And sometimes we choose things that aren't the best for us to self-repair. Right? And then, we see that with addictions, right?

Dr. Dave:
Yeah.

Tracy:
We see a lot of, "You know, what? I don't want to deal with that stuff. So I'm going to go over here and do this, so I don't have to think about this." Right? Because we've gone through all those stages and we are worn out, and we can't do anymore,

so we're just going to, at that point, self-repair. During all these things, our bodies are going through stuff with that. Right?

Dr. Dave:
Well, certainly. Yeah.

Tracy:
So we've got to figure that ... Okay, so what did ... You said a whole lot in that, and that led me to all of this trauma talk, because holy shit, my brain just went, "Okay, where are we going?"

Dr. Dave:
I was just being open-ended because I was thinking from a clinical context, but I was also thinking about, from the trauma that people experience in corporate America. And I could remember working for a very large organization in Chicago. Well, I could talk about them. They no longer exist. Arthur Andersen, Andersen Consulting. They no longer exist anymore.

Tracy:
What happened to Arthur Andersen? Why don't they no longer exist?

Dr. Dave:
Our government shut them down because they did some illegal stuff and they revoked their auditing license, so they couldn't ... Their core business was auditing, so they couldn't make any more money doing auditing, right?

Tracy:
Oh. Oh, wow.

Dr. Dave:
Yep.

Tracy:
Okay.

Dr. Dave:
Our Congress did that.

Tracy:
Okay. Hmm ... I did not know. All right.

Dr. Dave:
Yep, yep. So that's what happened to that organization.

Tracy:
Okay.

Dr. Dave:
But I remember one night we were working on these crazy projects, and this lady was just on her desk screaming. I had no idea, and we're all, they're working late and we're trying to figure out how to help her, and she was just screaming. And because I was a medic in the military, they automatically want me to go in there and go deal with what's going on. So I'm trying to talk to her, and she thinks that's ... She just lost it. And, you know—

Tracy:
So she lost her connection with reality? So she dissociate—

Dr. Dave:
With reality.

Tracy:
Right?

Dr. Dave:
Yeah, she totally disassociated. And then I saw her, either weeks or months later, and she was in a different space. I met this bubbly, chuck, "I'm going to run through this wall" individual,

to this person who was just like on her desk, screaming, freaking out like the world had ... There was something bad happening there. And then all of a sudden, I saw her, and it's probably the meds that were affecting the way she responded because she was more like a drone, you know? Or, I think—

Tracy:
She was in a heightened state when you, she was ready to knock down walls when you met her, and then she got to a breaking point. And then, the next time you saw her, she was very subdued.

Dr. Dave:
Very subdued.

Tracy:
Okay. Yeah.

Dr. Dave:
And I'm going like, wow, just going through that experience. As we were talking about disassociation and the trauma. And we never knew really what was the trauma, but working in those high-stressed type corporations...

Tracy:
Yep.

Dr. Dave:
... they'll break you.

Tracy:
Yep.

Dr. Dave:
They will break you because of the demand that they'll have on you. So it was just, and that's where my brain, the flight or fight.

Tracy:
Yeah. No, no, no. I get that.

Dr. Dave:
It's a thing.

Tracy:
We're going to come back to that, right?

Dr. Dave:
We'll come back to it.

Tracy:
That goes back to if she had had trauma, if she had trauma entering this position, and if she was in a place, because this is where someone could say maybe she had bipolar disorder, or maybe she had severe depression, or maybe she had mania, or maybe she, all of these clinical diagnosis, someone would ... Okay, she was at a really high point, and then she was at a breaking point, and now she's at a low point. Right?

If there had been trauma, there could've been a way that she masked how the trauma affected her by having this persona of "I can knock down walls." And then, she gets into this job where this causes undue stress on her, which activates a lot of what the trauma response is. And then, she has a breaking point and her brain cannot, her body cannot, her soul cannot do that anymore.

Dr. Dave:
Yeah.

Tracy:
And then she collapses. Right? So if we look at that trauma response, she collapses, and then she's going to figure out how to get out of that. And she was probably hospitalized or something like that—

Dr. Dave:
She was.

Tracy:
... and put on some meds. Right, right.

Dr. Dave:
Yeah. And then, she no longer worked there, right? She resigned.

Tracy:
And then, I wonder if the trauma was ever addressed. See, that's where sometimes the ... Sometimes there's a ... Today, probably not so much, but in the past, trauma would not have been addressed. We even talk about trauma amongst the races. Right?

Dr. Dave:
Yeah.

Tracy:
Because historically, we think of trauma as being shell shocked, as the war response to, or the effect, the psychological response to war because we've been through so much, we've seen so much as a war vet, then we've got this trauma response and that's acceptable, because then we expect it. But think about—

Dr. Dave:
Yeah, we could drag that into what we see happening in the inner cities, right?

Tracy:
I was just getting ready to say that.

Dr. Dave:
I'm sure that's where you were ... Yeah. Okay, you go girl.

Tracy:
Yeah. Because if we see how war affects the soldier, no one was looking at the parallel of living within a certain cultural community or a certain violent community where you see gunshots, knife stabbings, violence, domestic violence, every day as your norm—

Dr. Dave:
Every day.

Tracy:
... every day as your norm. And these particular people in this community have been diagnosed with so much shit. Instead of looking at, "Oh, they're kind of like a soldier going through all of this daily trauma. How do we help them with that and process that trauma?" We're getting so much better at right now.

Dr. Dave:
Yeah. Well, or even labeling, right? Because it's like, there's something wrong with these people why they can't deal with ...

Tracy:
Right.

Dr. Dave:
While I'm like, "Hey, just imagine if you had to live through that, what would you be like? You'd probably be like the woman that I worked with"—

Tracy:
Yeah, exactly. Exactly.

Dr. Dave:
... that ended up on that desk, screaming as if ... Something crazy was happening in her space at that time.

Tracy:
Yep. And I'm going to ask you to stop saying crazy—

Dr. Dave:
Yep, yep.

Tracy:
... because ...

Dr. Dave:
Did I say so something crazy happening?

Tracy:
You've said it five times probably in our conversation today.

Dr. Dave:
But I didn't call her crazy, right? I didn't label her as crazy. I just talk about the experience as crazy. I hope I did that, right?

Tracy:
Yeah, well—

Dr. Dave:
Okay, good.

Tracy:
Let's not use crazy.

Dr. Dave:
What term would you like to use? What paranormal term you would like to use?

Tracy:
Oh, wow. You just went there, didn't ... You just had—

Dr. Dave:
I didn't have to go there, right?

Tracy:
Paranormal. Wow. I'm surprised you didn't say, "What esoteric term would you like to use?"

Dr. Dave:
I'm just ... Yeah, you know?

Tracy:
No, people are just having some issues. It's really that. It—

Dr. Dave:
Yeah, having a hard time.

Tracy:
They're having a hard time, right? Because when we label it as crazy, then there's a certain expectation that you can't even talk to them. "She crazy," or "He crazy."

Dr. Dave:
Yeah.

Tracy:
Mm-mm [negative]. People just going through shit. And I don't know if we, and that forgiveness piece? The grace to be understanding with people, because we go through stuff, and we don't know how our stuff affects another person's stuff, and we don't always know how their stuff affects us.

Dr. Dave:
Yeah. It's a trigger.

Tracy:
Because we may not, we may not know what activates us. And I like to call it an activation.

Dr. Dave:
Ah Yeah. Activation versus the trigger, and yeah.

Tracy:
Yeah. The trigger warnings, as people call them. That can be triggering for people. Right. Because of aah.

Dr. Dave:
Yeah. Truly. Yeah.

Tracy:
Yeah. That's my paranormal term for trigger: activation.

Dr. Dave:
Activation. We'll use the word activation; that's for the trigger.

Tracy:
It's just a gentler term. Yeah.

Dr. Dave:
Yeah. Yeah. It's interesting, the type of training that you go through and the language that people use. Well, let's talk about experiencing healing in a community setting. To me, it's extraordinarily powerful and provides this opportunity to receive, as well as to give in the journey, really. As we're starting to develop this route before the truth, what has that been like for you as you're working through bringing healing in a community setting? Or, I could use a different word, group setting. Probably what I'm really referring to.

Tracy:
Yeah. Well, group and community are both good because we do need to educate the community that these things are going on so that they can be a little more aware of how they interact with people. I think the community that really needs work is the policing community.

Dr. Dave:
Yeah.

Tracy:
Having the policing community understand how this stuff affects people would be very helpful. How we can heal within the group community, or group setting. It goes back

to belonging, Dave. There's a lot of power in being in a group where you feel like you belong, and that that group is supportive in holding space. You can show up as you are, without the mask, and the performance, and the things that we do in order to protect ourselves from even feeling our own emotions. I think that groups can be very healing, and some can ... If the groups aren't led by a healed healer, they can be a little more destructive because we've got these wounded healers helping heal people, and wounded healers, good God. They're bad wounded healers. We're all wounded in some kind of way.

Dr. Dave:
Some way. Yeah.

Tracy:
It's the healer who's done the work so that they can support others in the work. And some—

Dr. Dave:
Yeah. So like—

Tracy:
Go ahead.

Dr. Dave:
Yeah. We were just talking about Resmaa [Menakem] and *My Grandmother's Hands*. He talks about the work that he has done with different police officers in trying to bring about healing throughout. So I mean—

Tracy:
Healing my community is important. People who have mental health issues that are not treated, that have been untreated, and their behavior may be, maybe displayed as a little aberrant for community. That's when the police are called in to handle these

situations when they may not be the right people to have come in, or they haven't been trained to understand if this person is having a psychological issue, or if there's really a threat for all of that. It could be a communication thing. I think the really, really helping to educate police who want to be educated, who will be on call for those calls, is what's important. I don't know if you can make a whole police department learn all this because they may not want to. The people may not be equipped to do the thing.

Dr. Dave:
Yeah. Well, I would see this as a partnership that would take place. Like what's happening in a lot of communities today, where you have an advocate who's partnering with a police officer, or couple of police officers, to help to deal with this. Look, it's a hard skill to learn. It takes years of practice to be able to work with someone who's activated by whatever it is that's going on in their lives in that moment. I like to look at it. Go ahead.

Tracy:
That's interesting that you said it takes years to learn. Having had very, very many, many psychology students, and training students to become clinicians and in internships, it can be learned. However, what I've seen is the most effective is for people who naturally have it. There are people who are—

Dr. Dave:
They're gifted that way.

Tracy:
... They naturally have that ability to hold space for people, to support people, to be there for people. I haven't run into very many people that I've trained who have had to learn the skill because they've got it.

Dr. Dave:
Yeah.

Tracy:
Right. Yeah.

Dr. Dave:
Okay. That's a very insightful perspective to look at that. Not only just in the context of police officers getting better at that, but in group sessions, where people are giving and receiving, where people are helping to heal each other in that space. I know that in some of the work that I'm doing with some of my corporate clients, we begin to see that. They're not only receiving in the process, but they're also giving in the journey as well, which is beautiful. Right?

Tracy:
It's huge. There's an accountability in that space. I worked with domestic violence perpetrators, and they're all men. To be able to work within that population, to me, was such a gift because how these men held each other accountable within the group setting was a beautiful thing to see. Right?

Dr. Dave:
Yeah.

Tracy:
It was a beautiful thing to see them heal from their own traumas in order to help support others to heal through their traumas. We didn't have a 100% success rate, but the rate that we did have of those who did do the work was really beautiful to see. In turn, they could see how their traumas were activated in their relationships. There was a parallel program, at one point, where the women who were the survivors, the partners of the perpetrators—

Dr. Dave:
The partner. Yeah.

Tracy:
... did work. The men did the work at the same time. Some of those couples, of course, reconciled and were able to be successful. Some were, "This is not a good space for me." It didn't happen. It was really beautiful to see that, and to know that in that kind of group setting, there could be healing. There was healing, and they did support one another. It was a really beautiful thing to see a bunch of dudes sitting around, crying, and loving up on each other, and supporting each other. Right?

Dr. Dave:
Yeah. Letting it out, because as men, we don't like to let it out. We won't let out. But, the fact that they could let that out—

Tracy:
Yeah.

Dr. Dave:
... so they can have that beautiful experience.

Tracy:
Sometimes the only emotion that you learn is anger, and you got to figure out how to deal with that and how to process it.

Dr. Dave:
It may not just be anger. It may also be suppression. The thing is, "Big boys don't cry. Big boys don't feel. What are you doing?" Those are the things that you may learn growing up in your home or in your community.

Tracy:
Right. Yeah. If not learned in your home, somebody's going to tell you, "Boys are tough."

Dr. Dave:
Yeah.

Tracy:
"Boys don't cry."

Dr. Dave:
"Boys don't cry."

Tracy:
"There's no crying in sports."

Dr. Dave:
"There's no whining either."

Tracy:
"There's no whining in sports."

Dr. Dave:
Knock it off. Yeah. Yeah.

Tracy:
Yeah. Very interesting.

Dr. Dave:
I'm thinking the root before the fruit. It's core to experiencing a sustainable—

Tracy:
I'm sorry. I have to say this. Every time you say "root before the fruit," do you remember John Witherspoon in [*Boomerang*], oh, my God, saying "the rooter to the tooter, that you eat the whole pig."

Dr. Dave:
Yeah. Yeah.

Tracy:
The rooter to the tooter. That's all I think about when I hear that.

Dr. Dave:
When you hear me say "the root before the fruit"?

Tracy:
They're rooter to the tooter.

Dr. Dave:
Oh, we're not doing the rooter to the tooter. We're doing the rooter to the fruiter.

Tracy:
Oh, my God. That's so dumb. Okay.

Dr. Dave:
What I'm saying is that, look, it's core to experiencing this sustainable mind, body, and spirit healing effect. That's what we're looking at. When there's no root, the healing will not stick. The individual becomes discouraged because of some of the failures that they may experience. What is that like when people doesn't have the ability to absorb and experience the healing so that it could be sustainable, that they could go off and do the work on their own? In the end of the day, even though you and I may have the best intentions and the best skills—

Tracy:
Yep.

Dr. Dave:
... it takes that individual, or that group, to go forward and do that work and make those changes. It's [the] only way healing happens. Let's talk about that a bit more.

Tracy:
Yeah. That goes back to the body. If one is grounded in their body, they can build and dig into their own roots. The body becomes that space of safety. When I'm in a space where my

body has betrayed me or has been traumatized or I have been holding on and suppressing, if it's not a safe place for me to be in my body, I'm not going to be able to do the work because my body is the root of all of the work. That's what grounds me so that I can do the work. That's the somatic part of healing. We have to do the somatic part of healing in order for healing to occur. It's like a tree. When I work with my clients to do the healing work, I actually go through a meditation before we do it.

I have them plant their feet down on the floor, and maybe hands on their knees, but I send them through a light meditation, and we go through the whole body. Then once we get to the feet, I have them visualize roots growing out of the bottom of their feet, moving through the floor, the basement, all the layers of the Earth, planted right into the core of the Earth. I sometimes say, "I want you to hear it kind of 'glink', like you've really touched the Earth, and you are grounded, and you are planted here, safely in your body." Then I have them pull their roots back up, but still stay tethered to the Earth. Then have them build a really big, beautiful bubble around their body, so they feel protected, and then also have them connect themselves to spirit, so that they're connected above and below, so that they are here grounded, yet they're still connected to the strength of spirit, so that they can do the work.

Dr. Dave:
Yeah.

Tracy:
That takes a lot of practice, Dave.

Dr. Dave:
Yeah. It takes a lot of work.

Tracy:
I agree, when you're escaping your body, your whole life.

Dr. Dave:
Yeah.

Tracy:
Even for men. Men are, "What the fuck are you talking about being in my body? What is that?"

Dr. Dave:
Yeah.

Tracy:
The first place they go, I don't mean to be whatever. The first place they usually go is right into the groin area. "That's where I'm grounded in my body." Right?

Dr. Dave:
Yeah.

Tracy:
I'm, "Come on. Really?" If that's what I got, I'm going to work with it. Right?

Dr. Dave:
Yeah.

Tracy:
I'm, "Okay, let's ground yourself in your, whatever, your testosterone"—

Dr. Dave:
Whatever it is.

Dr. Dave:
Whatever it is.

Tracy:
"Your space, whatever that space is, let's get grounded." Right.

Dr. Dave:
Right.

Tracy:
And to be completely honest, that's not a bad place to go. Because the root. So if we talk about an ancient old, here we go with the woo, woo, woo paranormal, as you call it. I don't think it's that at all. But I work with the chakra system. Right? So I work with the energetic system of the body. And the first chakra is the root chakra, which is at the base of the spine, which is where the prostate is living. That's where the prostate lives.

Dr. Dave:
Pretty much. Yeah.

Tracy:
That's right where the ... So that, to me, is the root. And if we go into the root of the person and get grounded in that root chakra, then we can do the work. And then we work up. We work up through the chakra, through the bottom.

Dr. Dave:
Well, that's the rooter to fruiter because that fruiter is produced the seed, which brings life. Right?

Tracy:
Well, I mean, it's the rooter to the tooter because the tooter's in the head, right? It's the nose. It's the snout to the butt. So it really is that kind of idea.

Dr. Dave:
I was just thinking about this one guy that was just coaching and dealing with the fact that he was just difficult. And it, just having conversation with him about being aware and mindfulness and what does it take to get there. And what's

causing him to have some of the challenges that he's having with people? One day he just came in, he goes, "Dr. Dave, I'm just not being very mindful at times. And this is something that I'm going to work on." I said, "That's a beautiful thing. I'm glad that you arrived at this space. And I can't wait to see what what's going to be next for you."

Then he spent him walking through it, beginning to learn more about just being aware about what he's saying, how he responds to other people. And it's not, he didn't mean anything bad, but the way he came off to ... And especially to some of the women that he was working with. Oh my God, they hated him. But over time, for him doing that work and coming to that realization, right? That he needed to be grounded in something. And he chose that. And so that was great to see.

Tracy:
Yeah. How you started that off, when you said this person I was working with and he was really difficult.

Dr. Dave:
Yes.

Tracy:
I even changed that verbiage. Because he was not purposefully trying to be difficult.

Dr. Dave:
Yeah.

Tracy:
He had behaviors that made it difficult for him to communicate with people.

Dr. Dave:
Or connect with people too.

Tracy:
Or connect with people. Right. And I would really, really want, I want people to reframe how they view ... Because what we do is if this dude is difficult and he becomes, I'm not saying you did this, but I'm just saying in general, right? I'm on label this cat difficult, which means it's a character flaw. So I'm going to judge it, and everything he judge, or that he does that supports my idea of him being difficult becomes even stronger. If I look at this dude that "whoa, he has some really, really difficult ways that he responds, which prevents him from connecting with people." Gives me a whole nother view of him. And maybe I can allow him some grace and I can be mindful of how I communicate with him.

Dr. Dave:
Yeah. Right. So that's the language of people describing him. Right.

Tracy:
Yep.

Dr. Dave:
Even though they see it as a behavioral issue, the language and the label is that this is a very difficult person to deal with.

Tracy:
Yeah.

Dr. Dave:
Yeah. So.

Tracy:
And to help him reframe that because I'm sure he's heard that. That he's difficult.

Dr. Dave:
I'm sure he did. Yeah.

Tracy:
And to say, "There must be some things that cause you to be activated," not you, this is what I would say as a clinician or a therapist. That "there's some things that you probably have experienced that causes you to respond in the way that would seem difficult to other people. Your response would seem difficult to other people." And then I would have him go, "Can you look at that from an observer lens and see when that happens?" And then he would be like, "Oh yeah, it happens this, this, this, and this." And I'd be like, "What is your body feeling when you respond?" That's the work right there. Because he'll be like, "As soon as somebody says something, my shoulders go up because I feel this tension in my body," and then we start working there.

Dr. Dave:
Right. So some of that stuff was driven from a cultural context for him and the way he grew up. But the way we did the work that we ... Our sessions were always walking sessions, and I intentionally took him outside and had the walking session to bring about a different energy for him. As opposed to that was being in a room and because at first we were in a room and then I'm like, "Yo, let's go for a walk." And that changes the whole dynamic of the conversation, how we listened to each other, how we responded to each other. So that was really powerful.

Tracy:
Yeah. Bravo for you.

Dr. Dave:
It didn't save his job just to let you know. But the fact is that he grew for the months that I saw him after his awareness. He grew tremendously and had a different relationship with others in the workspace.

Tracy:

Yeah. And maybe the goal wasn't for him, I mean the goal is to keep the job, but maybe his own personal journey goal was to not stay there and to be able to show his work somewhere else. And I applaud you for taking him walking. In Wisconsin, we have this beautiful Lake Michigan.

Dr. Dave:

Yep.

Tracy:

And Milwaukee has a beautiful lake front. And I walked with my clients many, many, many days. I even had a client, and it was 15 degrees below zero.

Dr. Dave:

Don't miss those days, Tracy.

Tracy:

Bruh. And this particular client, they wanted to walk no matter what the weather was.

Dr. Dave:

Yeah.

Tracy:

Because it was ... There's something of on going side by side with somebody where you don't have to look them in the eye that they just start ... Just, blah. And it was great. And it also is, it's a release. It's that body getting involved with the healing because the body's got to release too. And that's what walking helps them to do.

Dr. Dave:

Without a doubt. Without a doubt. Walking is just such a healing tool.

Tracy:
Yeah. Yeah. I've even gone running with clients, like a quick 15, 20 minute run, and then after the run, we do the session. It's beautiful.

Dr. Dave:
Yeah. I'll be on the ground. I'll be like a guppy out [of] water. A fish out of water.

Tracy:
Right.

Dr. Dave:
Yeah.

Tracy:
Yeah.

Dr. Dave:
Well, hey, let's wrap up. This has been an amazing conversation.

Tracy:
This is, yeah. I just start, you put a quarter in me today and it was just like ...

Dr. Dave:
And sorry for stacking questions originally. Because I just couldn't control myself. I'm like, "You know you're stacking questions." Right?

Tracy:
No worries. I think we got through at least two of them. I don't know if we got through all of them.

Dr. Dave:
We got through enough that we did provide enough value. So let me close and say thank you for listening to the *KnolShare with Dr. Dave* podcast. Our conversation today was about the root before the fruit. The rooter before the fruiter. Look, the healing

journey is difficult. I could tell you that. And so we have to have this intentional effort that will help us to develop deep roots so that there can be an abundance of fruits. Fruits produced in healing. So there's no shortcut. We must engage and do the work. So I hope this learning experience prompted you to seek to discover more ways to find your level of awesomeness.

That's what I want. And so just to give acknowledgement, the *KnolShare with Dr. Dave* podcast [is] streamed on Spotify, iTunes, Audible, and Google Play. Hello, Kayanna Brown Hendrickson. Thank you for dropping the music for this podcast. This podcast is copyright 2022 by Dr. Dave Cornelius and KnolShare.org. I am eternally grateful for the partnership that I have with my friend Tracy Treacy, who I have known for a very long time. And she said something very interesting. "You know, Dave, I have known you most of my adult life. Which is a good thing, so crazy."

Tracy:
Yeah. That is interesting. Isn't it? Wow.

Dr. Dave:
Wow.

Tracy:
That's a long ass time.

Dr. Dave:
No, it's a good ass time.

Tracy:
It's a good time. But it's a lot of years, bro. That's cool to maintain relationships with people that you've known 30-plus years.

Dr. Dave:
Yeah, yeah.

Tracy:
Wild.

Dr. Dave:
Yeah. It's called love.

Tracy:
That's what it is.

Dr. Dave:
That's what it's called.

Tracy:
That's exactly what it is. Yeah.

Dr. Dave:
Patience and kindness. It's called love.

Tracy:
Yeah. Yeah. And deep respect.

Dr. Dave:
Yes. Without a doubt. All of that.

Tracy:
All of that.

Dr. Dave:
Yeah. I just had a, I was reflecting there for a moment. I was thinking about the day of your wedding, that I was out playing softball in a white suit. On a softball field with your husband.

Tracy:
And on that note.

Dr. Dave:
See yah soon.

Tracy:
Peace out; we're done.

HEALING, THE ANTIDOTE TO TRAUMA: A CONVERSATION WITH DR. DAVE AND TRACY TREACY

Podcast: *KnolShare with Dr. Dave,* found on Spotify, iTunes, Audible, and Google Play

VLog: https://vimeo.com/704008260

Kayanna:
(singing)

Dr. Dave:
Hello, and welcome to the *KnolShare with Dr. Dave* podcast. This is Dr. Dave Cornelius, your host. We are continuing our great conversation of belonging and healing with my guest Tracy Treacy from D & S Healing Center.

Tracy:
Yay!

Dr. Dave:
Our topic today is healing, the antidote to trauma. Trauma is a source of pain that can be described and we can give it the name. So our conversation is going to really dig into forgiveness, somatic healing, psychotherapy, professional coaching, and spiritual healing. So Tray, Tray, Tray, how are you, man? What's going on?

Tracy:
You know, life is good.

Dr. Dave:
Yeah.

Tracy:
... good friend. Of course, it is. How are you doing?

Dr. Dave:
I'm amazing. I'm amazing and I'm jealous because I'm thinking about you hanging out at Coachella, which is a fun place to be.

Tracy:
Really. That's what we're doing?

Dr. Dave:
Well, that's not what we're doing, but I'm just telling your business so we can talk about it.

Tracy:
Exactly. That's wrong

Dr. Dave:
Belonging and healing.

Tracy:
Yes. Coachella was a good time.

Dr. Dave:
Awesome.

Tracy:
I mean, I would actually go back.

Dr. Dave:
Yeah, yeah.

Tracy:
Yeah.

Dr. Dave:
Yeah.

Tracy:
Yeah. It was a lot of people though, man, and it was fun.

Dr. Dave:
Yes, it is.

Tracy:
... COVID. It was a lot of people.

Dr. Dave:
But you were more glamping than anything else, right?

Tracy:
How do you ... What? No. I was not glamping.

Dr. Dave:
Yeah, you were. I didn't see you. You weren't sleeping in the tent or in your car.

Tracy:
No, no. That's more than glamping. I mean, they have yurts. Yurts. What are those things called? Yurts?

Dr. Dave:
Yeah. Something like that. Yeah, like ...

Tracy:
Yeah. The thing, that tent, the—

Dr. Dave:
The teepee thing?

Tracy:
The teepee tent, or the tent with the big opening at the top is ... I'm not going to call it a teepee. But it is a tent with a hard side. You know?

Dr. Dave:
Yeah.

Tracy:
And you could get one for the whole weekend. There's levels, and it started at about $4,500, and it went up to $7,500.

Dr. Dave:
Yep.

Tracy:
Wow. This is a real thing.

Dr. Dave:
Well, yes, it is a real thing. So did you have a sense of belonging as you were there?

Tracy:
I actually, yeah, because you feel even in that big crowd of people, you're all there for the same thing. So you belong to the place where people go to appreciate music. You go to really enjoy artists, to do their thing. You see the performers in their, all their glory, like this is what I was born to do. So you feel like you belong to this exclusive little club of over a 100,000 people and you have access to. Everybody's so very nice to each other. Because we, being a little bit older, there were some of us, but there's a VIP section, and then there's a general. So we were VIP and the general population folks, we were amongst them.

Dr. Dave:
Nice.

Tracy:
So it was really, yeah, it was just kind of cool. All the young folks acknowledging us, being like, "Look at you. You dope. You here! Yay!" So it definitely felt like I belonged.

Dr. Dave:
Okay. Well, that's what I wanted to just check in on. I just wanted to check in on that.

So we want to jump into the very first part of our conversation, the healing power of forgiveness. So I think of forgiveness as a powerful state of spiritual, mental, physical presence that allows every person to move beyond the trauma that they've experienced. We know that forgiveness is not easy because ... and oftentimes we want to just hang out in that comfortable space because trauma is something that we know and it feels good here.

So I was also looking at a quote, and some people attribute this to Buddha, that they talk about, "the lack of forgiveness," well, I'm paraphrasing, "can be something like having a state of mind of holding a grudge against someone which is like drinking poison and then hoping the other person dies." That's kind of a Buddha thing that I hung onto. So let's talk about the healing power of forgiveness and start there before we get into some of the other practices.

Tracy:
Yeah. It's a interesting one, Dave, because immediately, as you said, the pain of the trauma. You, sometime on some level, want more harm to that person than to forgive, if it's a person. In order to forgive the person or the situation or whatever for what has happened that has affected you, is a difficult route for people. Because I mean, you think, "Why should I forgive them when they hurt me?" It's a real, it's a process.

What I like to do, and I don't know how popular this is or how popular it will be, is begin with helping the person forgive themselves. Not for blaming themselves for it happening to them because that happens a lot too in the mind. It's, "Well, if I hadn't gone or if I wasn't there or if, or if, or I was just a little kid, I was defenseless, but maybe there was something wrong with me," that kind of thing. It's hard. It's really difficult. So to really focus on forgiving self and then others, I think is really important to do. There are steps to forgiveness. That's a whole nother podcast, but—

Dr. Dave:
Is it?

Tracy:
Yeah.

Dr. Dave:
I thought it was this podcast.

Tracy:
I mean, we're talking about a whole lot of stuff right now, right? The—

Dr. Dave:
I know. I got to talk about a whole lot of stuff.

Tracy:
So the steps of forgiveness is, there are stages just the grieving process.

Dr. Dave:
Yeah.

Tracy:
... those kinds of things. So, I mean, it may come up. But I'm talking in circles because it's just a very convoluted thing to do. Ultimately, we know that forgiveness is a release. It's a release from the body of however the trauma has affected you. And that is the goal because the stuff is stored on a cellular level and forgiveness helps to release that. And—

Dr. Dave:
Yeah. Well, without a doubt. Right—

Tracy:
Yeah. People go—

Dr. Dave:
Go ahead.

Tracy:
—"I can forgive, but I can't forget." And that's real because it's not about forgetting. It's about when I think about whatever happened, my nervous system doesn't respond at a level that it was before. So when I think about something and I'm at a 10, as I do the process of forgiveness and healing, when I think about it and it's at about a 1 or a 2, then I know that there is healing and forgiveness in that. But that doesn't mean you forget it.

Dr. Dave:
Without a doubt. It stays with you for the rest of your life in most cases. But thinking about the courage and empathy that's required to step into bringing forgiveness as a gift because I look at it in that context that when you are able to forgive someone for the traumas that they have brought into your life, it's a gift to not only yourself but also to that other person. It requires that you have the courage to give it a name, to really step in and have that conversation, and then empathy to look at the context of the perpetrator of trauma in your life, the context of the empathy: What was going on with that person? What's up with them? Why did they do this? And beginning to try to understand what that really means. So—another context of it.

Tracy:
Yeah, and I don't want our listeners to think that they have to confront someone to forgive them, that they have to extend the words, "I forgive you," to someone who has traumatized them. That's not always necessary—

Dr. Dave:
Agreed.

Tracy:
—because the end result is, who are you really doing it for is not that person. It's for you. If we look at it spiritually, the karmic laws and all of that talking about Buddha, then, yeah, there is a "what I put out, I get back" kind of thing. But that doesn't mean you haven't forgiven someone if they're not in your presence, because sometimes,

... Dave, that can retraumatize you to actually have to speak to the person. And what if the person has transitioned? So it's not always necessary to have dialogue with someone in order to forgive them. What you talked about, there's a compassion piece, and that is with yourself, the compassion and grace to have with yourself as you are going through that process because some people get in their hair, like, "I should be further than this. I don't know why this still affects me." All of that. Have grace with yourself so that you can go through that process and not judge yourself because of where you're at when you're healing, while you're healing.

Dr. Dave:
Right. Yeah.

Because healing is a journey. I call it a transformative journey, where we're trying to get to a place of a favorable outcome for oneself. This is just me going out and looking at how do we think about the pain in the trauma, and I try to think of it in two ways. I think of it in generative and limiting pain. Where we think that generative healing entails we're going through this pain, we're trying to find some healing in the process. That generative healing in itself gives us this opportunity for a favorable outcome that we're seeking. The same thing with we're dealing with pain and looking at some level of healing that we could get to a place where we are in a place, I'm sorry, where it's too pervasive and it's too hard. So we're dealing with generative and limiting type of healing as we're walking through this trauma.

What say you in terms of your experience with providing as a healer? You provide this space for generative healing and also the space for dealing with limiting healing because that is a reality where, "Oh, my God, this is too much. I can't deal with this. I have to put this in this box over here." And to me, I look at that as the limiting healing experience. But the generative would give us a way to like, "Okay, I could deal with this. Maybe incrementally." So let's talk about that.

Tracy:

Those two work together. I don't think they have to be separate of each other because that's about the grace piece. If today I wake up and I can't deal with this shit, then you honor yourself and you don't deal with this shit. If tomorrow I wake up and I'm like, "Well, maybe I can just chip at it a little bit," then you do it on the day you can chip at it a little bit. So I think they work. They're not separate because you do both within the process of healing. Give yourself the space and the support to do that and begin to understand what you need in order to support yourself while you're going through those moments.

So if it's the moment, the day where I can't deal with this shit, then what do I need today to support me so that I'm what I would call, to myself if I'm saying this, productive or getting some stuff done, but not letting that interfere with my world. Maybe it is getting, I don't know, whatever you do, it could be ... I like people walking around barefoot to ground themselves, and sometimes that irritates the hell out of people. But what that does is it helps you to connect, and when you're there with earth that helps to support. Maybe rocking, maybe dancing, maybe humming, maybe singing, maybe reading, maybe curling up in a fetal position for 20 minutes just to give yourself a hug. Do what you need to do and then continue your day.

What happens sometimes is people get into that freeze place when they say, "I don't want to deal with this today, or I can't. It's too heavy." Then they shut down and they don't do anything. And sometimes that's okay. I'm not saying we have to be machines. This world says, "If you're not doing anything, then you're lazy." Or, "The idle mind is a devil's playground," you know, all of that kind of stuff that we hear, those messages. Put those in a compartment; put those on the shelf and be like, "Well, today I need a little bit more support. I'm going to do that for myself. And then I'm going to continue my day." Then on those days where I feel like I can deal with this, "Today I might chip away at it a little bit and still support myself." So you're always going to need to support yourself and figure out what that means for you.

I think that's actually as difficult as the healing because when we're traumatized, we don't know how to support ourselves, because during the traumas, all we know how to do is survive in order to get out of it or in order to be okay. That, finding those things that help to soothe my nervous system can be as much of a struggle as healing some of the trauma.

Dr. Dave:

So that's the perfect transition period to something that's one of your favorite topics, like somatic healing. So we think of somatic therapy where it operates off the idea that what happens to you in life is stored not only in your mind, but also in your body. So as you were talking about walking around barefooted or curling up in a fetal position, I was thinking about somatic healing, and I know that's something that's one of your favorite topics.

Tracy:

Yeah. Because as I said earlier, it's how I think trauma is stored in the body, on a cellular level. If we feel it, and sometimes we are not connected with the body enough to feel where it is in the body that it's happening. So what trauma can be really good at is helping us to dissociate, so we disconnect from the body and when we can and get fully embodied and begin to feel what the body's telling us, then, not only then, but those are the moments where we have an opportunity to heal.

Like, in session, I will have a person sit and really just, it's almost as if I asked them to turn their eyeballs in so that they're scanning their body to see what's going on. Then if there's areas that they feel movement or whatever, I can help them focus on that area to see what kind of communication that area wants to share with them. This can be in forms of breath work. This can be in forms of meditation. This can be in forms of embodiment. There are ways to do it, to help the person begin to verbalize what's happening.

Some of the time can be taken away or can be used because people don't understand how to sit in their bodies because during trauma times they've learned how to dissociate. So maybe there is not a lot of trust in the body or maybe there's blame: "My body has caused me pain, or because of my body, this has happened," and all of that. So there's a dissociation.

To help them to feel safe enough to be in their body so that they can listen to their body is a process. So we're talking about building trust with me and then building trust with the body and then allowing parts of the body to speak to them and then seeing how that connects. So it's a process, a process, a process, and some of the ways to support that process is through somatic work.

Somatic work can span a lot of different things. We talk about energy work; we talk about healing touch, reiki. Those are some forms of somatic healing. Dancing is a form of somatic healing, getting in the body. Yoga is a form of somatic healing, being in the body. That reminds me, I got to get something to somebody. I build ... I know. I'm like, "Shoot, I forgot to send that email."

I kind of put together a yoga flow for the different chakras of the body because usually when we need to get in the body, we're focusing on the lower half, so from the solar plexus to the lower half of the spine, solar plexus to the base of the spine, because I think I've talked about the chakras. There's seven chakras in the body, and we focus on the lower three to really get into the bottom because foundational work, root work, old family work, all of that, creativity is in those lower, how I feel about who I am. I built a series of yoga positions, asanas, to do in sequence in order to help support those areas, so that we can get into the body to heal. My gosh, Dave, there's so many different kinds of embodiment work that can help with the somatic healing that I think is worth researching with people. Some people don't need or want to go there in order to heal because they can do their process a different way. And that's okay. I don't want people to think that "oh, I got to do somatic work in order to heal." It's available for whoever can benefit them and not everybody does.

Dr. Dave:
Yeah.

Tracy:
Massage is another way, right? So it's about releasing the body of ... It's like releasing the body of toxins after you have a wonderful night of drinking or not so wonderful night of drinking.

Dr. Dave:
We don't do that.

Tracy:

We don't do that. No. And you wake up the next day and you've got your lemon water to help detox. You're drinking tons of fluids that is releasing, getting rid of toxins. You're sweating the stuff out. That's how I look at rum. You got to sweat it out somehow.

Dr. Dave:

Yeah. Got to get it out.

Tracy:

Sometimes. Yeah. Especially if there's some disease in the body that it's like "let's start to work some of this stuff out of the body," if we're holding it.

Dr. Dave:

I was thinking about something that Jamie Foxx said, but I'm not going to say it in this podcast, "you got to blow that shit out," right?

Tracy:

I mean, you do. Interesting that you said it because sometimes when people are doing their process, they may have diarrhea, they have explosive gas, they may be throwing up. That is also a way of getting some of this stuff out.

Dr. Dave:

Yeah. He was talking about it. I figured I'll get you to spit the water out as we were talking. But psychotherapy healing also is another form of healing. Which we call talk therapy, right?

Tracy:

Yeah.

Dr. Dave:

It's working with a trained therapist, deep conversations with inquiry, how is that also helpful as a healing tool?

Tracy:
Someone being ... That's so interesting. It was similar last night. I can't even remember, but someone was talking about their partner being an emergency room doctor in their residency and asked me what I did for work, and I shared that I was a psychotherapist, and they're like, "So you got to with what ED doctors deal with. You don't know what you're going to get on any given day; how do you deal with that? Because that takes a lot of mental work." And I said to him, "My job, I don't even think of it as my job, my role in what I do and how I support people is to hold space."

Dr. Dave:
Yes.

Tracy:
And when you have someone that is, you feel it. And I do this virtually and I hope my clients can feel it that I am there for them 100% in that moment. And when you have an audience that is holding space for you, where you feel safe, that helps healing. It really helps for you to be able to share what you're feeling and not be judged and ridiculed, and to be given witness to, and honor that what you're saying is simply it is, and it's important and I don't question it. And when that's provided for a person, that's like "oh, wow." So yeah, that's very helpful.

Dr. Dave:
It is.

Tracy:
It depends on the psychotherapy. Also there's different kinds, but you're going to ask something because I can keep going with it.

Dr. Dave:

I just wanted to make sure that we cover it as a topic and an available form of healing because also, we have professional coaching, right? Which emphasizes getting the individual or group to their desired destination. We're thinking that ... You know, the culture itself believes that each person is whole and capable of finding a desired solution through exploration and discovery while working with a coach. I know that something that you're exploring, that's the work that I do. So I would just like to dig in a little bit more into that as a source of healing as well.

Tracy:

Yeah. I think coaching is a ... It feels to me as if with therapy, I'm holding space; with coaching, I'm digging. I'm also digging with therapy, but I'm digging to connect. With coaching, a person has a goal and you say, "If this is the goal, let's do the goal backwards and see what you need to do to get to the goal." There're different ways of doing that and to hear their goal, and to support them in that causes healing.

Dr. Dave:

Yes.

Tracy:

That helps them to be accountable, that helps them to have ... It's almost like you're partnering with them to do what they need to do.

Dr. Dave:

It is partnership.

Tracy:

Right. So you've got that partner, you've got that person. It's not handholding; it's support. It is "I'm going to help you get to where you are going to get to, and if there's glitches in it and you find yourself falling short, that might be a therapy issue and not a coaching issue." So it's being able to tell those things apart too.

Dr. Dave:
Yeah. And it's important because ... You know that I was coaching someone, I said, "Oh my God," I got to a point where I know that this was beyond my capability. So I'm like, "Hey Tracy, would this person be a good referral for you?" So that's also part of the responsibility of coaching. Because besides holding space, it's thought partnership of helping those individuals to move forward in their journey to wherever they want to get to.

Tracy:
Yeah. I was coaching with someone, and there were some issues going on that could have used a therapist. But that wasn't my role in that moment. So in that moment, because of all of the crisis that was going on, it was like, "Okay, so let's look at what you do well, right? And let's help you apply that to what you want to do." So it's about transferable skills and how those will help you, so to get that person out of the mindset of the crisis, so that they can begin to see that yeah, they've done some really good things in their lives. It's not all of this trauma that has got them to where they are. It's all the good stuff and how they've supported themselves that can help them in their career.

Dr. Dave:
Yeah. It's getting beyond those limiting beliefs. "I can't do, I am not good enough." It's really looking at helping them to shine and lighten those great skills that they already have within themselves. To help them to move forward to their destination. What about spiritual healing? So, we think about spiritual healing, we're talking about meditation, prayer, you

kind of talked about touching with healing intent. Some people may have a communication with a higher being or a spiritual realm to facilitate healing within the individual or in groups. So I know you bring some aspects as a healer of spirituality to your practice as well to your clients.

Tracy:
Yeah. You mentioned meditation and that can be a spiritual approach to healing. Right?

Dr. Dave:
Yeah.

Tracy:
When I heal or as I do my work, I work with spirit. I work with, I call God Spirit, Big Guy, Big Gal, you know, the presence of the Light, right? That has brought into however, I do what I do. All the time, every day. So I do my best to connect. And when I'm working with someone and they feel that, "You know, I should pray more or I should meditate, or I've got no spiritual practice" etc., this is where we can also say, "Well, what are the things that you have done?" And then help them to recognize that some of those things are spiritual practice.

That they may be doing it already. And they don't realize that connection and taking care of yourself can be a spiritual connection because that is showing appreciation for who you are and that you can show up for you. And then maybe connecting that to a source if people believe in that. And if I connect that to source, then that can help me get through some of those limiting times where I feel like I can't do this shit. Let me connect the source and get grounded in source so that I can have the energy I need to move forward. Sometimes if you don't—a habit for yourself, connecting to source can help you do it.

Dr. Dave:
That's for sure. So, we kind of walk through different options for healing, from forgiveness, to somatic, to psychotherapy, to professional coaching, and spiritual healing. I'm going to try and be funny here. Was Coachella a form of healing?

Tracy:
You are really on one today. Actually, yes it was, thank you very much, because it healed some of the COVID trauma to actually see people out and about having a good time. Yes.

Dr. Dave:
Okay.

Tracy:
See, I can make it work.

Dr. Dave:
I knew you could, so that's what I put it in there. Now, is there anything else you would want to add in as another source of healing besides the ones that we covered today?

Tracy:
Since this is about belonging, even though family can be really jacked up, family can be a really good source of healing. Right?

Dr. Dave:
Yeah.

Tracy:
Like the people that you connect with can be a really great source of healing. And that doesn't mean you have to use them as your therapist, or your coach, or your source. That means I can show up authentically in my stuff, and not be judged by these people who love me. They will allow the grace, and the space, and the patience, and the compassion, and the love, to support me through this, so that I can feel okay doing it. "I

don't have to do this. I don't have to be ashamed. I don't have to be embarrassed. I don't have to hide. I can show up, and these people will still love me for me."

Dr. Dave:
Yeah. I am so glad you brought that up because just sharing a story with my relationship with my son, that him showing up, and moving here with us is a form of belonging and healing for him, because he just said that last night, we were out having dinner, and he expressed that, because he said he's the prodigal son. I said, "Yeah, but I'm the prodigal dad." So that we are able to create space such that he could find healing and acceptance, as he's going through his journey. No, I'm glad that you brought that up. It kind of touched me and is right at home for me as a topic, as a dad, and also for our relationship. We rub each other, but we have great love and respect for each other and for our own family, for our families.

Tracy:
Yeah.

Dr. Dave:
Right?

Tracy:
Yeah, and that feels like we belong. We belong to each other.

Dr. Dave:
Yeah, we do.

Dr. Dave:
Yeah, so I hope to see you when I go see your son play in a couple weeks. You know we come out here, and she goes like, "No, I'm going to Southern France."

Tracy:
Oh no, I don't know. I'm going to go to New York and see him play, so I don't know.

Dr. Dave:
Yeah, yeah.

Tracy:
Maybe.

Dr. Dave:
Well, we're going to see him play in a couple weeks.

Tracy:
Good, good. We told him. We told him.

Dr. Dave:
Yeah. So, I'll be pinging you, I'm like, "Can I get some VIP connects?"

Tracy:
We told him that. I was like, "Dave said he'll get his tickets, but he wants to be treated as a VIP." And Dylan was like, "What does that even mean?"

Dr. Dave:
It means like I get to go backstage and feel like I belong. I get to meet the artists and feel like I belong.

Tracy:
Oh, all of that. Yeah, you'll get that.

Dr. Dave:
Yeah, that's what I'm talking about.

Tracy:
And if you go backstage, though, you might become a roadie. So I don't know if I would go backstage.

Dr. Dave:
I don't know about all that. "No, I'm not moving your drums. Sorry."

Tracy:
Oh my gosh, yeah. Is it ... That's a part of it.

Dr. Dave:
I know.

Tracy:
Wow. I mean, it's exciting, but it's a lot of work.

Dr. Dave:
Yeah, it is. Yeah, very much so. A lot of somatic skills needed to move those drums, right?

Tracy:
Yeah. Well, we're talking about him, I guess I can give a shout out to the artist.

Dr. Dave:
Yeah.

Tracy:
How tacky would that be?

Dr. Dave:
Yeah.

Tracy:
Yeah. Amber Mark is the artist.

Dr. Dave:
Nice.

Tracy:
And she is awesome.

Dr. Dave:
Good.

Tracy:
She's super awesome. Yeah. You ought to check ... Have you listened to her music?

Dr. Dave:
Yeah. And I played it for Dave and said ... This is my son, Dave. I was like, "Hey, we're, we're going to go and check out this artist for your mother's birthday." And he was super hyped. So ...

Tracy:
Awesome.

Dr. Dave:
Yeah. Yeah.

Tracy:
Yeah.

Dr. Dave:
So it's going to be good.

Tracy:
Yeah. She's a wonderful, wonderful young woman.

Dr. Dave:
Nice. Well, let's let me end our conversation for today and just say thank you for listening to the *KnolShare with Dr. Dave* podcast. And the conversation that you had was about healing, the antidote to trauma. And we know healing is a difficult journey. No shortcut. Got to do the work. Got to do the work, and put the time and energy into that. So I hope that this learning experience will prompt you to seek more, to discover ways of finding your level of awesomeness.

The *KnolShare with Dr. Dave* podcast is streamed in Spotify, iTunes, Audible, and Google Play.

The music for this podcast, intro and outro, was created by my niece, Kayanna Brow-Hendrickson.

This podcast episode is copywritten 2022 for Dr. Dave Cornelius, and KnolShare.org. I just always wanted just give a big love and shout out to Tracy for bringing her knowledge and experience to this conversation, and sharing this back to our audience and the world. So Trace, thank you.

Tracy:
You are welcome. Thank you for asking me. This was good. Yeah.

Dr. Dave:
Yeah. I think we have like ... Yeah. I like it. It's lots of fun. Love it.

Tracy:
Lots of fun. It is lots of fun. Yeah. Yeah. Thank you. Thank you, Dave. I appreciate it.

Dr. Dave:
Very much so.

Kayanna:
(singing)

ABOUT DR. DAVE CORNELIUS, AKA "DR. DAVE"

Dr. Dave Cornelius, aka "Dr. Dave," is a business, executive, and organizational coach, partnering with leaders and teams in for-profit, startup, and non-profit organizations to deliver a level of awesomeness that meets their goals. He works with Fortune 50 to Fortune 500 companies, helping them to deliver more than $1 billion in customer value. Dr. Dave is a coach to university researchers to facilitate the commercialization of their startup ideas and bring them to market.

Dr. Dave delivers in-person and virtual immersive learning experiences in agile (Scrum, Kanban, SAFe, etc.), design thinking, lean startup, and professional speaking. His doctoral manuscript focused on "The Value of Scrum to Organizations" in support of his management and organizational leadership doctoral path. He also holds a BS in computer science and an MBA.

Dr. Dave is a big community contributor and the founder of the Agile for Humanity conference and meetup that supports the BIPOC community to have a voice in the product development and technology fields. He is the founder of the 5 Saturdays STEAM program that empowers under-estimated high school students to pursue knowledge and careers in STEM fields.

He is the author of five books (*Transforming Your Leadership Character: The Lean Thinking and Agility Way, Elastic Minds: What are you thinking?, Prayers to my Abba Father God, Belonging and Healing,* and *Deliver Value*).

You will find his monthly podcast and blog, *KnolShare with Dr. Dave,* on popular streaming services as well as KnolShare.org.

He is a husband, dad, and grandfather.

REFERENCES

Baldoni, J. (2017). *Fostering The Sense Of Belonging Promotes Success*. Forbes.
https://www.forbes.com/sites/johnbaldoni/2017/01/22/fostering-the-sense-of-belonging-promotes-success/#3846d15510f2

Buettner, D. (2019). *A 'blue zones' diet: Live longer from what you eat*. CNN.

Coqual. (2020). Median belonging score by race and gender. Belonging series part 1. Retrieved from https://coqual.org/

Creary, S. (2019). *Beyond Diversity: How Firms Are Cultivating a Sense of Belonging*. Knowledge at Wharton.
https://knowledge.wharton.upenn.edu/article/belonging-at-work/

Diamond, L. (2013). Sexual-Minority, Gender-Nonconforming, and Transgender Youths. Elsevier Inc.

Evans, F. (2022). *When Abraham Lincoln Tried to Resettle Free Black Americans in the Caribbean*. Retrieved from
https://www.history.com/news/abraham-lincoln-black-resettlement-haiti

Glassdoor Team (2021). *What Is Diversity, Inclusion and Belonging?* Glassdoor for Employers. Retrieved from
https://www.glassdoor.com/employers/blog/what-is-diversity-inclusion-and-belonging/

Global Industry Analysts, Inc. (2021). *Diversity and Inclusion (D&I) world market report*. Retrieved from https://www.strategyr.com/market-report-diversity-and-inclusion-forecasts-global-industry-analysts-inc.asp.

Grant, A. (2022). Twitter post.
Retrieved from
https://twitter.com/adammgrant/status/1478399527723970564?lang=en

Harari, Y. N. (2015). *Sapiens (A brief history of humankind).* Harper Perennial.

Herway, J. (2018). *How to Bring Out the Best in Your People and Company*. Gallup.
https://www.gallup.com/workplace/232958/bring-best-people-company.aspx

Hougaard, R., Carter, J., and Marissa Afton, M. (2021). Connect with Empathy, But Lead with Compassion. Retrieved from hbr.org.

Huppert, M. (2017). *Employees Share What Gives Them a Sense of Belonging at Work. LinkedIn Talent Blog.*
https://business.linkedin.com/talent-solutions/blog/company-culture/2017/employees-share-what-gives-them-a-sense-of-belonging-at-work

IDEO U. (2019). Designing strategy course.

Kennedy, J. T. and Jain-Link, P. (2021). *What Does It Take to Build a Culture of Belonging?* Retrieved from HBR.org.

Kotter, J.A. (2014). Accelerate (XLR8): Building strategic agility for a faster-moving world. Harvard business review press.

Nittle, N. (2021). *The Link Between Psychopathy, Narcissism, and Racism*. Retrieved from https://www.verywellmind.com/.

Noah, T. (2019). *Born a Crime: Stories from a South African Childhood*. One World.

Parker, K. and Horowitz, J.M. (2022). Majority of workers who quit a job in 2021 cite low pay, no opportunities for advancement, feeling disrespected. Pew research Center. Retrieved from https://www.pewresearch.org/fact-tank/2022/03/09/majority-of-workers-who-quit-a-job-in-2021-cite-low-pay-no-opportunities-for-advancement-feeling-disrespected/

Porter, M. E. (1996). *What is strategy?* Retrieved from HBR.org.

Shellenbarger, S. (2018). *Why Perks No Longer Cut It for Workers*. Wall Street Journal. https://www.wsj.com/articles/why-perks-no-longer-cut-it-for-workers-1543846157

Srikanth, A. (2021). *New study finds white male minority rule dominates US*. The Hill. Retrieved from https://thehill.com/changing-america/respect/diversity-inclusion/555503-new-study-finds-white-male-minority-rule/.

Stall, L, (2022). Comedian Trevor Noah on humor and belonging. CBS News 60 Minutes. Produced by E. Alexandra Poolos. Associate producer, Collette Richards. Broadcast associate, Wren Woodson. Edited by Joe Schanzer. Retrieved from https://www.cbsnews.com/news/trevor-noah-the-daily-show-60-minutes-2022-06-19/

Twaronite, K. (2019). *Five findings on the importance of belonging.* Retrieved from www.ey.com.

Valencia, Richard R. (1997). *The evolution of deficit thinking: Educational thought and practice.* The Falmer Press/Taylor & Francis.

Made in the USA
Las Vegas, NV
23 August 2022